RUGBY UNION

The Skills of the Game

RUGBY UNION

The Skills of the Game

BARRIE CORLESS

THE CROWOOD PRESS

First published in 1985 by
THE CROWOOD PRESS Ltd
Ramsbury, Marlborough,
Wiltshire SN8 2HR

This impression 1998

British Library Cataloguing-in-Publication Data

A catalogue record for this book is available from the British Library
ISBN 1 85223 768 6

Dedicated to Dianne, Louise and Emma for their support

Picture Credits

Photographs are reproduced by kind permission of the following:
Northampton Mercury (figs 6, 7, 31, 34, 35, 36, 41, 43, 66, 67 and 97);
Roy Peters (figs 18, 19, 23, 24, 28, 39, 59, 74, 92, 93 and 98); Damian
McFadden (figs 17, 25, 26, 29, 44, 48, 49, 65, 68, 86 and 87); David
Gibson (figs 52, 53, 54, 55, 56, 57 and 58); Gloucester Citizen (figs
71, 72, 73 and 88); Pete Jenkins of Picturesport Associates Limited
(figs 20, 21, 22 and 27); Martin Lovatt (frontispiece and fig 30); Clive
Mason (fig 61); John Courtney (fig 69); other photographs are by
Andrew Purssell of Rugby School.

Typeset by Inforum Ltd, Portsmouth
Printed in Great Britain by The Bath Press

Contents

Barrie had a distinguished playing career for Birmingham, Coventry, Moseley and England. Previously the R.F.U. Divisional Technical Administrator (Midlands), he was later Director of Coaching at Northampton Football Club, and played a big part in that club's rise to the top of the English game. He became Director of Rugby at Gloucester F.C. in July 1993. He has extensive coaching experience at home and abroad, and has produced a coaching video for the R.F.U. He has also contributed to *Get Ready for Rugby Union* (The Crowood Press Ltd 1989).

From a successful International career to one of the most respected and innovative coaches in English Rugby, Barrie Corless has become an 'authority' on all aspects of Rugby Union.

His success both on and off the field has been second to none. A coach with an exceptional vision and understanding for the game and more recently a Director of Coaching who masterminded one of the most astonishing success stories at Northampton F.C.

There are not many former internationals who become successful coaches. Barrie Corless is certainly one of them. The resurrection of Northampton Football Club is in no small way due to him.

In this book he emphasises the basic skills of the game for both forwards and backs. Young players are his main target and all possible encouragement must be given to the youngster with an interest in the game – the lifeblood of the sport we all so love.

The book is easy to follow and puts over in simple terms the skills required to improve. There is also an important stress on the decision-making process – a vital ingredient for all players, whatever their position, which, allied to a high level of skill, produces a successful team.

Rob Andrew
Wasps, England and British Lions

This book helps highlight the importance of appreciating the needs of the individual within a team environment and offers a unique insight into both Northern and Southern hemisphere coaching techniques with an emphasis on 'decision making'.

Dick Best
National Coach

Barrie Corless is well known throughout England as a thoughtful and innovative coach. His coaching book gives a good grounding in the basic skills of the game for both forwards and backs and is an ideal book for players of all ages.

The coaching drills included provide a much needed library of skills practices for the teacher and coach where variety within a coaching session is so important.

Wayne Shelford
Northampton, North Harbour and New Zealand

1 Introducing the Game

APPROACH

Rugby football can be a confusing game for beginners. Most young players when they arrive for their first games lesson at a school or mini-rugby club will have little idea of what is involved. Unlike soccer or cricket, it is unlikely that they will have taken part in impromptu games on the local park or playing field. True, some may have watched *Rugby Special* and will have learned snippets of the laws from the excellent commentaries of Bill McLaren, but most will have watched the action with little idea of what the players are trying to achieve.

I can remember my father explaining the rudiments of the game to me before I entered grammar school. I was unable to comprehend how a team could make any forward progress when the ball could only be passed backwards; I had never seen a game of rugby football in my life, which made it even more difficult to understand. From the teachers' and coaches' point of view this may be an advantage. Young players will arrive much as I did, with no predetermined idea of styles of play, tactical formations or even the position in which they may want to play. On the other hand, for many people the thought of introducing rugby football to youngsters is quite daunting with its complicated, oft changed laws, and such difficult facets of play as line-outs, scrums, rucks and mauls.

It is important to stress from the first lesson that rugby football is fun; many youngsters will be apprehensive about contact activities and sympathetic teaching in the early stages is essential. After all, the majority of youngsters during their play will indulge in many physical contact activities – wrestling, fighting, rolling about and so on; this should be to our advantage. The attitude of the teacher and coach in this early stage of a player's development is most important. Players should be encouraged to learn, to make decisions, to make mistakes and to learn from them. The fact that they are making progress and that the team performance is improving should be more important than the result.

Young players should play a form of rugby football from the very first lesson; there can be nothing more frustrating to a young lad who is eagerly awaiting his first experience of rugby than to find that he spends a complete lesson running up and down the field learning how to pass the ball or indulging in activities which have little relationship to the game itself. Small-sided games in well-defined areas of the pitch between boys of the same size is surely a more enjoyable and interesting way of introducing the game and of maintaining the interest of our young players for the future.

The coaching of team games has become a very complicated science in recent years. I often wonder if the players understand what many coaches are encouraging them to do. A great deal of time has been spent on unit and team skills, often to the detriment of the individual performer. The emphasis in this book will be very much on the individual, trying to show ways of improving individual skills, thereby making each player in the team a more competent performer and therefore more able to contribute to the team effort.

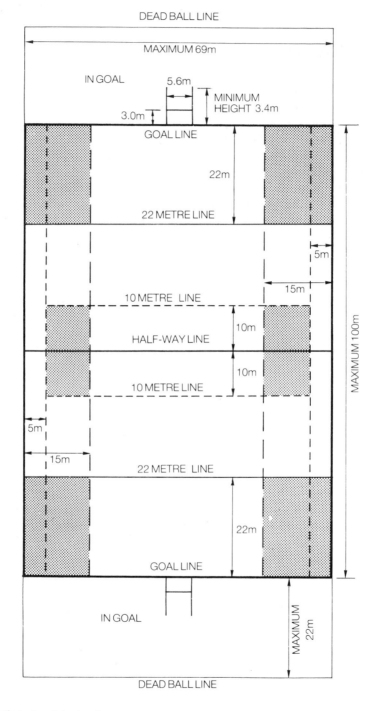

Fig 1 Dimensions of a rugby pitch, showing grid areas for coaching purposes.

Grids and Channels

The coaching grid is quite simply an area of the playing field which is divided up into equal size squares. For young players, seven or eight metre squares would suffice, with ten metre squares for older schoolboys or club players.

The rugby pitch itself is full of areas which may be used as coaching grids *(Fig 1)*. The advantages of using a coaching grid are that it helps the organisation for coaches, particularly when confronted with large numbers of players, it allows the pursuit of purposeful learning activities by a large number of players in a relatively small area, and it is flexible — grids can be combined to provide pressure practices, one group competing against another in order to test the development of a newly acquired technique. For continuous practices in order to encourage support play a number of grids may be combined to form a channel system.

Grids may be permanently marked on an area of the playground or perhaps a spare part of the playing field if one exists, but if the pitch is to be used, a better system would be to use cones or corner flags in order that the area can be moved regularly to safeguard the playing surface and also to overcome the problem of a confusion of additional lines. This method of teaching allows a large number of players to be involved in enjoyable competitive activities in easily defined areas where the coach can see them, control them and make the necessary coaching points as he moves from grid to grid. Working with groups of three to five players in each grid ensures that every player has a greater opportunity to handle the ball and to become involved in the practice, thus sustaining his interest.

Small-sided Games

I have already stressed the importance of using small-sided team games in the early stages of a player's development. If the coach can develop a series of games with simple rules in a relatively small area of the pitch then there will be ample opportunity for players to develop their running and handling skills. They will score tries or points in a variety of ways, becoming totally involved in the game. Rules will be developed in such a way as to be simple for the players to understand, and fitness will be developed because of the type of activity in which the player is involved.

A look into other coaching books from soccer, basketball and volleyball will unearth a multitude of games practices which will be of value. Below are a few of the small-sided games which I have found most useful in the teaching and coaching that I have carried out. They are of value as games in their own right in the early stages of a lesson, or possibly for more experienced players as warm up activities.

Corner Ball

Size of pitch One or two grids.
Teams Four versus four, five versus five, or six versus six.
Aim To touch the opposition with the ball while held in two hands.

Rules
1. Players may not run with the ball.
2. Defensive players may run anywhere within the grids to avoid the ball.
3. Having passed the ball, attackers may move to a more advantageous position.
4. Attacking players pass the ball around in order to touch an opponent with the ball held in two hands.
5. When players are caught they can:

Introducing the Game

a) join the chasers,

b) wait outside the grid and rejoin game after a dropped pass, or

c) do an exercise, for example five press ups and rejoin game.

6. Game ends when:

a) all opposition have been caught, or

b) time is up, i.e. most opponents caught in two minutes wins.

Spin and Chase

Size of pitch One grid.

Teams Two versus two.

Aim To make the highest number of passes in a given period of time.

Rules

1. Players may not run with the ball.
2. Ball may be passed in any direction.
3. No contact.
4. Dropped pass, possession goes to opposition.
5. Opposition obtain possession by intercepting a pass or from a dropped ball or ball going outside the grid.

Variations

1. Players may run with the ball.
2. Team making ten passes scores a try, twenty passes two tries, etc.
3. Conditioned passing, i.e. above shoulder height, below waist height.
4. Allow one versus one contact, i.e. an opponent may go in and wrestle for the ball.
5. Ball must be passed within three seconds.
6. Any combination of the above.

Tag

Size of pitch One grid.

Teams One versus three.

Aim Player with ball held in two hands tries to touch opponents with ball.

Rules

1. Ball must be held in two hands at all times.
2. When touched by the ball, opponent becomes the chaser.
3. Players may run in any direction within the grid.

Variations

1. Players when touched complete an exercise and rejoin the game.
2. Players when touched, crouch down and are released by players from their side picking them up.
3. How many opponents can the ball carrier touch in a given period of time?

End Ball

Size of pitch Two grids.

Teams Four versus four.

Aim To pass the ball to a catcher standing beyond the end line of the grid.

Rules

1. Players may pass in any direction.
2. Cannot run with the ball.
3. Must pass within three seconds.
4. No contact.
5. Ball must be caught cleanly for score to count.
6. Must stay within grids.
7. Opposition obtains the ball by:

a) intercepting passes,

b) dropped ball, or

c) ball or player outside grid.

Variations

1. Can run with the ball.
2. Must pass when touched.
3. Tackling introduced.

Corner Spry

Size of pitch One grid.
Teams Six players per team.

Rules
1. Players line up as in *Fig 2*.
2. Ball carrier (1) passes to and receives from each member of the team in turn.
3. When last player (6) has ball, player (1) runs round team and touches each corner of the grid in turn and returns to receive a pass from player (2) who has taken his place (*Fig 3*).
4. Repeat with each team member.
5. First team to complete the above wins.

Rugby Contact

Size of pitch – across a rugby pitch between the 22m and half-way lines.
Teams – maximum of ten versus ten.
Aim To score a try over opponents' line and to introduce contact.

Rules
1. Teams no more than five metres apart.
2. Player in possession runs to score or until held and tackled by opponents.
3. Holding or tackling allowed.
4. When held or tackled, player rolls ball between legs to team-mate.
5. No passing except by player receiving ball from between the legs of tackled player.
6. Six attacks per team unless:
   a) try is scored, or
   b) possession is held in tackle.
7. Restart after score by pass from centre.
8. No kicking.

Variations
1. Allow one extra pass per team.
2. Allow a player to maul the ball from his tackled or held team-mate.

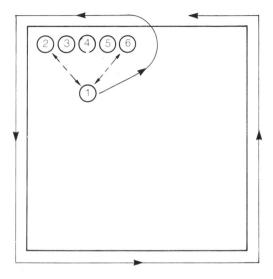

Fig 2   Corner spry.

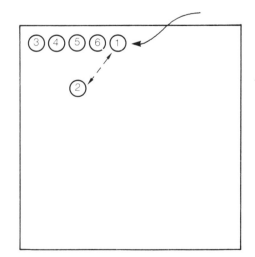

Fig 3   Corner spry.

INTRODUCING CONTACT

One of the questions that I am continually being asked when conducting coaching sessions for teachers is how to introduce contact in a safe and enjoyable way. I think it is important that all contact practices contain an element of fun, the use of small-sided games in grids for example. Equally important is the control of size and speed. Players of similar physique should be grouped together and the speed of players in the early stages of learning contact should be limited.

On the one hand, therefore, we have to make use of young players' enjoyment of physical contact, but at the same time acknowledge the fact that they may be apprehensive when confronted by a player running at speed with the ball.

Speed in contact is a difficult problem; it can be a cause of injury to young players when they are not sufficiently experienced to have developed the correct technique of the tackle, but may also cause problems for the ball carrier who may lose control of the ball at the moment of impact, thus depriving his side of the possibility of continuing an attacking move. I think it is important therefore in the early stages to control the running speed of the players. This can be done either by limiting the area in which the players are moving, making sure that the distance between the two opposing sides is kept to, say, five metres so that the player in possession of the ball has little opportunity to reach full speed before contact, or to make the player decrease his speed before impact by, for example, picking up a rugby ball or by a change of direction around a cone. The speed at impact is reduced and the technique is therefore more likely to succeed.

Contact activities should be included as part of every warm-up session. This provides the opportunity to develop confidence, to revise previously learned techniques and to teach new skills.

Warm-up Activities

Lifting and Turning (Fig 4)

Players in grids approximately eight metres square in groups of five. Four players (nos. 2, 3, 4 and 5) facing outwards. The other player (no. 1) lifts and turns each one in turn to face the centre of the grid. It is important to lift using legs and not back, i.e. bend legs, strong arm grip, straighten legs, lift and turn opponent. Repeat with all players.

Pass and Maul

A player in each corner of the grid facing into the middle. Player in the middle passes the ball to each player in turn, runs and wrestles for approximately five seconds to regain possession. A contact and strengthening activity.

Turn and Maul (Fig 5)

Player (1) passes to (2) who turns his back to become opposition. Player (3) runs and turns (2) as in 'Lifting and Turning' (above), trying to keep player (2) as upright as possible to expose the ball. Player (4) wrestles the ball free and passes to player (5) as in 'Pass and Maul' (above). Player (5) turns his back and opposes. Practise in any direction round grid in random order. Encourage the players to take a turn at all the activities.

2 v 2 Contact Game

One player from each team stands two metres in from opposite sides of the grid. The player in possession of the ball tries to run towards his

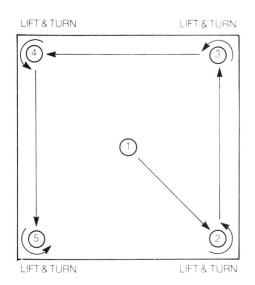

Fig 4   *Lift and turn warm-up activity.*

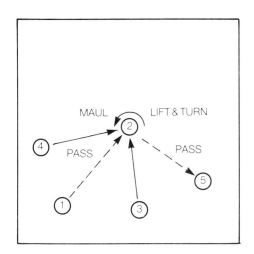

Fig 5   *Turn and maul warm-up activity.*

stationary team-mate and *hand* him the ball. His opponent tries to stop him by tackling or holding. The ball carrier must release the ball when tackled or held for his opponent to continue play. After a score the ball is handed to the opposition, play being continuous. Frequent changes of possession and much close quarter contact make this a tiring but enjoyable game. Change the players' roles regularly.

CONTINUITY AND BALL RETENTION

Screen Pass

The ball carrier uses his body to screen the ball from the opposition and at the same time holds the ball out for a supporting player who cuts close and drives on past the opposition.

Checkpoints

1. Drive into the opposition with the shoulder and stay on feet.
2. Push ball away from body towards the supporting player.
3. Receiver cuts close and takes the ball from the ball carrier with an aggressive forward driving movement leading with the shoulder.

Practice for Screen Pass (Fig 8)

Four players (X1 X2 X3 X4) stand approximately four metres apart as defenders. Four opposing players (O1 O2 O3 O4) run in close support. The ball carrier (O1) adopts forward driving position leading with right shoulder – body protects ball from opponent. On contact, ball carrier attempts to drive forward for a stride while presenting the ball to supporting player. Players *must* stay on their feet. Initially, defenders attempt to stop the ball carrier but help to

Fig 6　Wayne Shelford (Northampton and
New Zealand) illustrates a good body
position in contact.

Fig 7　Tim Rodber (Northampton and
England) driving hard and low from a
scrum.

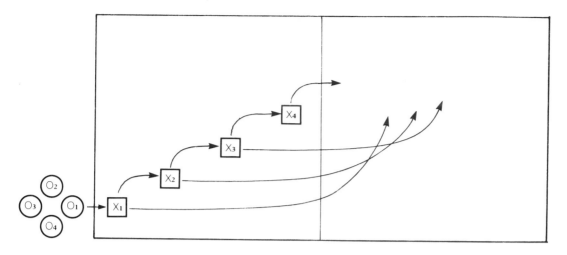

Fig 8   Screen pass practice.

keep him on his feet. As the technique improves, defenders can adopt a more aggressive role. Support players also adopt forward driving body position, leading with arm and shoulder to secure ball and drive on to the next defender. The practice is continuous, each player running to support or defend as necessary. Ball carriers should use both shoulders when driving.

The Maul Pass

This would be used when the ball carrier found it difficult to move the ball away to the supporting player. It is necessary in this instance for the supporting player to move in close and take the ball from the ball carrier.

Checkpoints

1. Ball carrier drives into the opposition with his shoulder and stays on his feet.
2. Support player leads with the opposite shoulder to the ball carrier and puts two hands on the ball.
3. Support player rips ball away from the ball carrier, turns and drives forward.

Note There may be occasions when the supporting player may not be able to drive

forward and continue the movement himself. In this instance, he should look to pass the ball away to the next supporting player thus continuing the movement.

Practice for Maul Pass

Same organisation as in 'Practice for Screen Pass' (above). Ball carrier (O$_1$) makes contact and presents ball to supporting player (O$_2$) who moves in to secure ball and prevent opposition from reaching ball. Note that if ball carrier leads with right shoulder, supporting player leads with left shoulder thus they provide a protective wedge round ball. The supporting player (O$_2$) then takes the ball and feeds O$_3$ who drives into the next defender (X$_2$) supported by O$_4$ and the progression continues with O$_1$ and O$_2$ in support. The sequence of activities is:

1. Contact and present ball.
2. Secure ball.
3. Feed.
4. Drive, etc.

Contact Game

Using the width of the pitch a series of small-sided games (six to eight-a-side) can be played simultaneously, taking care neither to use common touch-lines nor the goal-lines to avoid accidents.

Teams line up five metres apart. The attacking side's ball carrier runs to try to break through the opposing ranks. Defenders hold or tackle the ball carrier. Body positions as in the screen pass. The nearest support player secures the ball as in the maul pass and feeds to a free player who runs to score. Allow four to six attacks – if no score or the opposition are unable to win the ball from a tackle or handling error, change the attacking side. Encourage all players to run with the ball.

The Rugby Continuum

Recently introduced by the Rugby Football Union, the Rugby Continuum provides a well structured series of steps from a non-contact game at under 7 years to full-contact midi-rugby at under 12 years. At the end of this period of time young players should be well versed in the skills of Rugby Football and able to progress to the full 15-a-side game. Here is a breakdown of the main points from the continuum. For more details, consult the RFU pamphlet Rugby Continuum.

Stage 1: Non-Contact Mini Rugby Under 7

1. The teams shall not be more than 5-a-side.
2. The object is to score a try over the opponents' goal line.
3. All re-starts are with a free pass – the starter team must be behind the ball, the opposing team 7m away.
4. Initially players may pass the ball in any direction, but gradually encourage players to pass sideways and backwards.

5. Tackles are made with a two-handed touch below the waist of an opponent, a touched player must pass within three strides.
6. A player touched in the act of scoring a try shall be awarded the try.
7. Referees may help the players by calling 'tackled' when a player has been touched.
8. If a player is legally touched and fails to pass, the ball goes to the opponents.
9. When the ball goes out of play, a re-start takes place at the point where the ball or player went out of play.
10. Players must not hand off.
11. Players must not kick the ball.
12. The game takes the form of 2 halves of 10 minutes each.

Stage 2: Non-Contact Mini Rugby Under 8 – Additional rules

1. Teams should not exceed 7-a-side.
2. A team losing possession of the ball must retire 7m from the point of restart.
3. The ball can *only* be passed backwards or sideways.

Stage 3: Midi Rugby Under 9

1. The game is played between teams of 9 players, 3 of whom will form the scrummage, 6 of whom will form the backline. Positions should be interchangeable.
2. If the ball is passed forward or knocked on an uncontested scrummage is awarded.
3. Any player running with the ball can be tackled as laid down in the laws of the game.
4. If the ball is not playable *immediately* after a tackle, an uncontested scrummage is awarded to the team not in possession before the tackle.

5. The scrummage will be made up of one row of three players. The team putting the ball into the scrummage must be allowed to win the ball. Opponents cannot strike or push.

6. The backline of the team not putting the ball into the scrummage must remain 7m behind the scrummage until normal play resumes, except the scrum-half who must remain behind the hindmost foot of the forwards.

7. The game will be made up of 2 halves of not more than 15 minutes.

Stage 4: Mini Rugby Under 10 – Additional rules

1. All the laws of the game pertaining to the U-9 scrummage shall apply, except that the scrum half of the non-putting-in team must remain behind the hindmost foot of the forwards until play resumes.

2. A two man line-out is introduced extending from 2 to 7 metres from the touch-line. One player throws the ball in, whose immediate opponent must stand within the 2m line. One player stands ready to receive the ball from the line-out (ie a scrum-half).

3. The team not responsible for taking the ball out of play shall throw in the ball.

4. The off-side line for all players not participating in the line-out shall be 7m back from the line of touch. Players must remain behind the off-side line until the line-out has ended.

Mini Rugby Under 11 – Additional rules

1. At this stage the game will start with a kick off from the centre of the field. The kicker's team must remain behind the ball. The receiving team must be 7m back from the ball.

2. Scrummages are contested.

3. All the normal rules of play relating to kicking will apply. A player may not fly back at the ball indiscriminately. After a try has been scored, a conversion kick from in front of the posts may be attempted.

4. After a try or goal has been scored, the game will be re-started with a drop kick.

Stage 5: Midi Rugby Under 12

1. Teams will be made up of 12 players, 5 forwards and no more than 7 backs.

2. The laws of the game of Rugby Football Union will apply *except:*

Scrummage

1. The locks forming the second row must bind to each other with their inside arm and with their outside arm around the hips of the props.

2. The scrum-half not putting the ball in must remain behind the hindmost foot (off-side line) until the ball has emerged from the scrummage. In the event of a strike against the head, the scrum-half who has put the ball into the scrummage must not follow the ball until it is out.

Line-Out

1. The line-out is made up of two, three or four players from each side plus the player throwing the ball in and the latter's immediate opponent who must stand in the 2m area, and one player from each side in a position to receive the ball.

2. The line-out will extend from 2 to 7 metres from the touch-line.

Others

1. A player may not hand off an opponent in any way (a free kick re-start).

2. A game will be made up of two equal halves of 20 minutes.

2 Basic Skills

HANDLING

Confidence in handling a rugby ball is most important for successful, enjoyable rugby football. Every training session must therefore contain some handling practices, initially to learn the basic techniques of catching and passing the ball and later to pressure these techniques by using opposition. Young players should take every opportunity to improve their handling skills, by practising a variety of methods of transferring the ball, above the shoulders, below the waist, behind the back and so on, until the ball can be passed quickly and accurately from almost any position. A great deal of time is wasted at the beginning of a practice session as players hopefully kick at goal or aimlessly punt the ball around the field. Players should take this opportunity to improve their handling ability. A ball may be rolled or grubber kicked along the floor and then picked up, kicked into the air and caught before it bounces or passed quickly between groups of two, three or four players. Coaches should encourage their players to engage in purposeful activities with the ball as soon as they take the field. This can be achieved more easily if the coach is ready as soon as the first players arrive, and organises some individual skills practice. Too many coaches wait until all players arrive before starting, thus losing valuable opportunities of working with small groups of players. The following handling exercises are designed to introduce the basic techniques giving coaching points for player and coach, and then to progress to small game activities to test the skill development. Where appropriate, suggestions are made to help coaches to develop their own practices.

Handling Relays

To encourage as many repetitions as possible, I adopt a shuttle relay formation, i.e. teams split into two equal groups who face each other twenty-two metres apart.

The teams work continuously until all players are back in their starting positions. Relays are ideal for young players because:

1. They are competitive.
2. They are an easily organised warm up activity.
3. They allow reinforcement of previously learned techniques.
4. They are an ideal vehicle for repetition of new techniques.

Examples

1. While running, transfer the ball from one hand to the other behind the back before passing to next player.
2. As above but transfer the ball behind head.
3. As (1) but transfer ball under right/left/both legs alternately.
4. Pick up a stationary ball, run five metres and place ball on floor for team-mate to pick up.
5. As (4) but *roll* the ball for a team-mate to pick up the moving ball.
6. Fall on the ball, regain feet and place ball on the floor for a team-mate to repeat.
7. As in (6) but roll ball for team-mate to fall on the moving ball.
8. Run forward, throw ball into the air, catch

and pass to team-mate.

9. Any combination of the above.

Note In relays number 5, 7 & 8, a grub kick or punt may be used with more experienced players to replace a roll or throw.

Picking up the Ball (right hand)

Checkpoints

1. Place right foot close to the ball.
2. Bend knees.
3. With right hand behind ball, sweep ball into left hand.
4. Straighten knees and drive away.

Note Reverse the above if using the left hand.

Falling on the Ball

Checkpoints

1. Fall beyond and close to the ball.
2. Pull ball to chest with hands.
3. Protect body by turning the back towards opponent.
4. When ball is secure, get to feet and move away as quickly as possible.
5. Avoid spectacular dives to the ball.

PASSING

I have already stressed the value of quick, accurate passing of the ball to a successful rugby side; the ability to handle the ball with confidence is extremely important in the development of unit and team play. This confidence is built up through a succession of well-structured practices in which a player's newly learned technique is continually put to the test in small game situations.

The Lateral Pass *(Fig 9)*

Checkpoints

1. Hands out as target, fingers spread, thumbs up.
2. Pass ball into the hands of the receiver.
3. Receiver takes ball early, swings ball across body to complete the pass.
4. Use eyes to watch ball and look at target for the pass.
5. Run straight.

Young players must be encouraged to keep running while catching and passing the ball – this is helped by keeping the hips facing forward and merely turning the upper body towards firstly the passer of the ball, and secondly to the receiver of the pass. By encouraging the players to put the ball in the target and use their eyes, they will soon develop the rhythm of catching and passing on the run.

Exercise 1

In groups of three, shuttle backwards and forwards across a grid, passing the ball continuously.

Exercise 2

Organisation as in the first exercise. This time as each end player in turn receives the ball, he changes direction quickly. This means that the middle player is constantly turning and receiving very quick passes, thus testing his ability to catch and pass the ball a number of times very quickly.

Exercise 3

In fours, shuttle backwards and forwards across a grid. Two players are being pres-

Fig 9 *A good example of a player providing a target for the passer. Note how both players keep their eyes on the ball.*

sured in the middle of a group of four. The key coaching points are exactly the same. The players should be encouraged to pass the ball across the group and back again before they reach the end of the grid. Once again the pressure on the middle two men can be increased by the end players changing direction as soon as they have the ball in their hands.

Exercise 4 (Fig 10)

The group of four players in formation as in *Fig 10*. X_1 and X_4 are stationary, two metres from the end line of the grid. The ball is passed from X_1 to X_4 and back again by players X_2 and X_3 who are shuttling backwards and forwards across the grid. Players X_1 and X_4 may have to move their positions slightly in order to receive a backward pass from players X_2 and X_3.

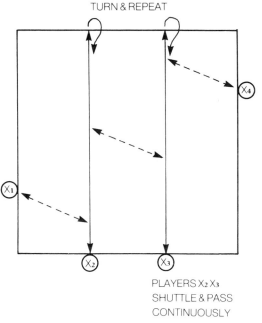

TURN & REPEAT

PLAYERS X_2 X_3
SHUTTLE & PASS
CONTINUOUSLY

Fig 10 *Lateral passing drill.*

Exercise 5 (Fig 11)

To encourage quick passing from the players. X₄ shuttles backwards and forwards across the grid and receives and returns a pass in turn from players X₁, X₂ and X₃. Player X₄ is encouraged to take the ball early and pass it back as quickly as possible.

Exercise 6 (Fig 12)

The players align themselves side by side at one end of the grid. The aim of the exercise is for the ball to be passed from X₁ to X₄ who scores a try at the far end of the grid before X₁, running behind the group, touches him with two hands. The object of this simple practice is to further increase the pressure on the handling of players X₁, X₂ and X₃. The players should be encouraged to run forward at speed as well as transferring the ball quickly from player to player.

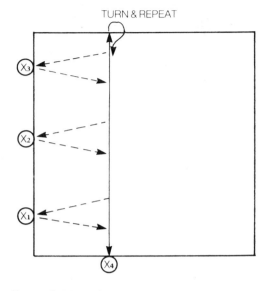

Fig 11   Quick passing drill.

Exercise 7

As *Exercise 6* except that player X₁ starts in front of the group and, after passing the ball to X₂, runs across in front of the group and attempts to put two hands on the ball carrier. The players are trying to score a try at the far end of the grid as before. This will lead to the introduction of the dummy pass as the defender may be tempted to run quickly across the grid without first of all making sure that the ball carrier has passed the ball. The three attacking players in this instance must be encouraged to keep their eyes on the defending player as well as being aware of the positioning of the player to whom they are about to pass the ball. This is an interesting exercise and helps to increase the players' awareness of what is going on all around them which is very important in the full game.

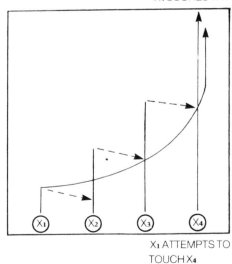

Fig 12   Opposed passing drill.

Basic Skills

Checkpoints

1. Players must use their eyes to be aware of the positioning of the defender and the receiver of their pass.
2. Ball carrier must run forward at speed in order to commit the defender.
3. Pass must be timed so that the defender is committed to the ball carrier thus creating an overlap.
4. If the defender carries on past the ball carrier, a dummy pass may be executed.

Committing the Defender

Having at this stage introduced a defender, it is important that players are aware of how they can commit the defender thus creating an overlap. The defender should be positioned in such a way that the attacking side are always able to exploit the overlap in the early stages. As the players become more confident in their ability to commit the defender and time the pass, so the defender can increase the pressure by either running more quickly or standing closer to the attacking players.

Exercise 8 (Fig 13)

Two versus one. Two players stand side by side at one end of the grid with the ball on the floor two metres in front of one player. The defender stands half-way across the grid opposite the ball. As soon as the first attacking player touches the ball the defender can move towards him; the attacking player times his pass so that the exercise is completed by the spare player scoring a try on the overlap.

Many players, even those quite experienced, think that they have to get very close to the defender in order to commit him. This is not so; in fact if the ball carrier gets too close to the

defender, the defender may be able to get a hand to the ball thus stopping the pass to the spare man. The *speed* of the ball carrier is important; if the ball carrier runs quickly, the defender has to run quickly to cover him and is therefore not able to change direction easily to cover the extra man.

Checkpoints

1. Carry the ball in two hands.
2. Look at the defender.
3. Run *quickly* towards the defender.
4. As the defender moves towards you, pass the ball to the spare player.

When the players are proficient at timing their pass, then the starting position of the defending player may be varied; for example he may start opposite the spare player or he may start

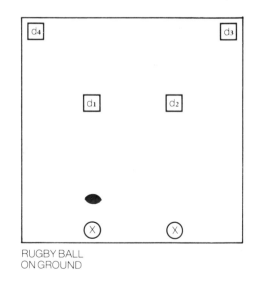

RUGBY BALL
ON GROUND

Fig 13   Two against one, showing alternative starting positions for the defender.

between the two. The ball carrier should run very quickly forward, thus committing the defender, and pass the ball to the spare man at the appropriate time. Once again, I stress the importance of the ball carrier running forward at speed, making it difficult for the defending player to change direction as he is also having to move at speed. The attacking players are thus becoming aware of how to beat a defender from a variety of different starting positions.

Exercise 9 (Fig 14)

Three versus two. The players are organised as in *Fig 14*. This allows more time for the three attacking players to perform their skills and builds on the two versus one exercises which have already been completed. Attacker X_1 picks the ball up from the floor at which time

defender d_1 moves towards him. The defender is committed and the ball passed to player X_2. As soon as X_2 receives the ball, defender d_2 will move forward to challenge him. The defender must be committed and the ball passed to player X_3 who scores a try. The tendency for young players when confronted by a defender coming from the side is to tuck the ball under one arm and to run in a wide arc away from the defender. Players should be encouraged to keep the ball in two hands and to run slightly towards the defending player thus preventing him from taking a line to cover both players *(Fig 15)*. This manoeuvre also preserves space on the outside for the remaining player to gather the ball and score a try. As the players become proficient at this exercise, once again vary the starting positions of the two defenders thus presenting the attacking players with different situations to

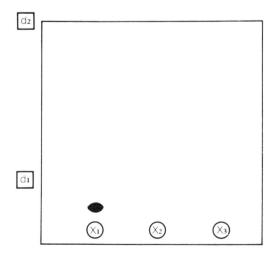

Fig 14   Three against two; starting positions.

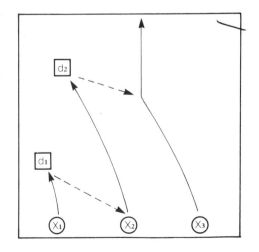

Fig 15   Three against two; running lines.

Basic Skills

overcome. All I say to players at this stage is 'score', and allow them to try to solve the problems their own way, only giving advice or reinforcing coaching points previously made where necessary. Remember the simple rules – carry the ball forward at speed, commit the defender. If there is no defender in front, run to score, if a defender comes towards you, commit him and pass the ball to the player in space. An interesting variation of the theme three versus two is for the players to react quickly to a changing defensive formation.

Exercise 10 (Fig 16)

Three versus two. The three attacking players line up with the ball in front of the middle man. The defenders take up positions opposite the outside two attacking players and are numbered 1 and 2. If no. 1 is called, that defender

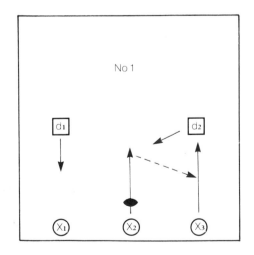

Fig 16   Three against two; decision making practice.

will move forward thus indicating that that part of the field is covered. The attacking player will pick up the ball and attack defender no. 2 in a two versus one formation as covered previously. If no. 2 is called, he moves forward and the process is reversed with the attacking players running at defender no. 1. In this exercise the attacking players will not know which side is to defend and have to react instantly to the new formation which presents itself to them.

Exercise 11

The formation is the same as in *Exercise 10* except that the attacking players have their backs to the defenders. Defender 1 or defender 2 will move forward thus indicating to the attackers when they turn round that that part of the field is covered and the attackers respond by picking the ball up and running to attack the other defending player in a two versus one formation as before.

Having covered the use of an overlap, encouraging the players to commit the defenders and transfer the ball to the spare man on their side, thus scoring tries, I think it is important to put them into situations where they have to create their own overlaps – in other words three versus three and four versus four where they will be encouraged to carry out a variety of manoeuvres in order to try and free a man on their side.

In the early stages of this practice, it may be advisable to stagger the defenders slightly so that the attacking players have a little more time in which to transfer the ball and support the new ball carrier. One common fault of the game at all levels is that players when passing the ball will stand and watch what happens on the outside of them rather than react immediately by supporting the new ball carrier. A side should go onto the field with the mental attitude of trying to outnumber the defenders at all times. The pressure initially can be taken off the attacking players by getting the defenders not to move until the man opposite them has possession of the ball, or complete one, two or three press-ups before moving forward, or stagger themselves so that each defender is a little further away from the man whom he is marking. This exercise should be conducted as a game. The three or four attacking players are encouraged to play against the three or four defenders to score a try, attempting to commit the defenders and, having passed the ball to a fellow attacker, run and support in order to try to outnumber the defenders. New techniques such as switch pass, a miss-out or a loop can be encouraged at this stage. These will be explained in more detail in the following section.

Having reached this stage players should now be confident handlers of the ball with an awareness of how to commit defenders, how to create an overlap and should be developing an appetite to score tries. It is important not to push on too quickly and, when necessary, to repeat an earlier stage. Many of the early exercises are ideal warm-up practices and useful revision of work carried out in previous sessions. Small games are competitive and with a variety of starting positions for the defender, should give the coach sufficient ideas for a number of rugby sessions.

HANDLING VARIATIONS

Having become proficient at the orthodox lateral pass and mastered the ability to commit defenders and time the pass to players in space, it is necessary now for players to increase their repertoire of handling skills. Passes such as the loop, a change of direction with a switch pass, or missing a man out, are useful skills in creating an extra man, for use when straightening a threequarter line or to change the direction of an attack.

The Loop

An easy method of creating an extra man is to use one player in the threequarter line on more than one occasion: having passed the ball, the player loops around the receiver and takes a return pass linking with those outside him to create an overlap.

Checkpoints

1. Pass the ball and follow (loop round the receiver) to take a return pass.
2. The receiver runs straight before giving a return pass to the first player.
3. On taking the return pass, first player links with those outside who have drifted wide to create an overlap.

Note There are two ways of giving the loop pass:

1. Turn towards the receiver so he sees the ball continuously and takes an early pass *(Fig 18)*.
2. Turn away from the receiver so he takes the ball wider and later *(Fig 19)*.

In my experience, the first method is particularly useful from scrums as the attacking side are under more pressure from defenders and have less time in which to complete this manoeuvre. The second method is useful from line-outs as the defenders are further away and will have time to drift to cover the extra man coming into the line. It is important therefore that the player giving the pass to the looping player runs straight and commits the defenders to him, thus stopping the drift.

Fig 17   Rob Andrew (Wasps and England)
calling for a 'mark' after making a good
catch.

Fig 18 The loop, turning towards the receiver.

The Scissor or Switch Pass
(Fig 20)

Uses

1. To straighten the line.
2. To change the direction of an attack.
3. Penetration to breach the opposition defence.

Checkpoints

1. Ball carrier runs slightly across the field and turns to show the ball to the receiver.
2. The receiver cuts close to the ball carrier and takes the ball out of his hands and accelerates.
3. Receiver must run straight.

Fig 19   The loop, turning away from the
receiver.

The Miss Pass

Uses

1. To miss out a closely marked attacking player.
2. To move the ball quickly to an unmarked player.
3. Used with an extra man joining the three-quarter line to create an overlap.

Checkpoints

1. The passer must continue running forward before passing the ball in front of the player to be missed out.
2. The player being missed out runs slightly towards the passer of the ball thus stopping defenders drifting to mark the overlap.

*Fig 20   Rob Andrew and Jeremy Guscott
perform a switch pass.*

The Scrum-half Pass

The scrum-half is a key man in any side. He is the link between the forward unit and the threequarters and he must be able to transfer possession won by the forwards with a quick and accurate pass. Any time taken by the scrum-half in the form of a step or backswing in the pass will allow the opposition backs to gain valuable ground to tackle their opposite numbers. To play a full part in the team, the scrum-half must master a variety of skills; kicking, running and tackling are essential, but the scrum-half's game stands or falls by his ability to give a consistent pass.

The Standing Pass
(Fig 22)

This is the basic pass for the scrum-half. Its main advantage is that it allows him to remain on his feet to support other players and to arrive quickly at the breakdown.

Basic Skills

Fig 21 *Phil de Glanville (Bath and England) shows good timing of the pass.*

Checkpoints

1. Back foot is positioned close to the ball.
2. Weight over the ball initially, knees bent, body low.
3. Front foot points towards the target, slightly in front of the ball.
4. Ball is scooped from the ground, the hand behind the ball providing the power. *Avoid picking the ball up and a time-wasting backswing.*
5. As the ball is passed the front foot moves towards the target as the body weight moves from the back foot. This helps to add power to the pass.
6. The hands finish pointing at the target.

In the early stages of learning the standing pass, scrum-halves can pass one-handed, sweeping the ball from the ground into the

Fig 22 *Robert Jones (Swansea and Wales) executing a standing pass.*

Fig 23   One-handed scrum-half passing
practice.

hands of the receiver. This overcomes the problem of picking up and slowing down the movement of the ball (Fig 23). To improve the passing of a player with a backswing, place a succession of rugby balls next to a wall or bench and get the scrum-half to execute his pass. The barrier behind the ball will stop any backward movement of the hands. To produce the spinning 'torpedo' type of pass, the hand behind the ball rolls over the ball at the moment of release. This type of pass travels through the air quickly but may require a slight adjustment of the hands on the ball before passing. In the early stages speed and accuracy are the most important features of the scrum-half pass. Length will increase as the technique improves.

Fig 24   The scrum-half dive pass.

The Dive Pass (Fig 24)

Once again, speed and accuracy are vital aspects of this pass. The dive pass is most useful when the scrum-half is under pressure from the opposition. The scrum-half becomes a much more difficult target when executing a dive pass as he is moving away from the opposition.

Checkpoints

1. Back foot behind the ball.
2. Hands on either side of the ball pointing at the ground.
3. Transfer weight and pivot over the front foot — drive forward and up towards the target.
4. Sweep the ball away and release with a flick of the wrists. Keep the arms back for as long as possible before release.

The well-executed dive pass looks spectacular, but players should avoid hurling themselves high in the air; this can result in a slow pass.

The Pivot Pass (Fig 25)

A useful variation for the scrum-half is the pivot pass which allows the player to use his dominant hand, thus giving his outside-half more time and room. The pivot pass is given with the scrum-half's back towards the opposition; otherwise the technique is as already described for the standing or dive pass. The pivot pass is most commonly used from a line-out on the left touch-line when the scrum-half wants to use his right hand. He should position himself a few feet to the infield of the catcher and face slightly towards the touch-line. As the ball comes, the scrum-half pivots on the right foot until his left foot faces the target. It is important that the outside-half makes an adjustment when receiving the pivot pass as it takes longer to execute than the orthodox standing or dive passes. The outside-half may stand slightly deeper or delay his run until the ball is almost in his hands. The pivot pass may also be used from a scrum on the right-hand side of the field to pass the ball to the outside-half positioned infield.

Practices for the Scrum-half Pass

Grid with five players. Each player in turn acts as a scrum-half and carries out the practice using both right and left hand. The four non scrum-halves position themselves near each corner of the grid as a static target for the scrum-half. With young players the target men may need to move closer.

Practice 1

The ball is on the floor in one corner of the grid. Using one hand only, the scrum-half sweeps the ball from the ground into the hands of each player in turn. The target players place the ball on the floor after receiving the pass.

When competent at moving the ball away quickly, the scrum-half uses his other hand to give added control to his pass. The dive pass can be practised using this formation also.

Practice 2

Passing to a moving player. The scrum-half positions himself half-way along one side of the grid; the other four players line up on the opposite side of the grid. On a command from the scrum-half each player in turn moves forward to receive a pass. The players return the ball to the scrum-half and rejoin the group. The players must not move too early or the scrum-half's pass becomes too flat or even forward.

Fig 25 Steve Bate (Wasps and England) illustrating the pivot pass.

Fig 26　David Elkington (Northampton)
showing excellent dive passing technique.

Fig 27　Dewi Morris (Orrell and England)
dive passing from a scrum.

Fig 28   Scrum-half practice – successive
quick passes.

Practice 3 (Fig 28)

The scrum-half makes a series of passes in quick succession. Four balls are placed five metres apart along a line. The scrum-half moves forward and passes each ball in turn to a different player who catches the ball and places it on the floor. The players line up ready for the return sequence using the scrum-half's other hand. As the passing improves, pressure can be increased by placing the balls closer together.

Practice 4

Alternate dive and standing pass. Two scrum-halves stand ten metres apart, each with four rugby balls. Four players line up to receive a pass from each scrum-half. Player A executes a dive pass, player B a standing pass. The players then change groups and complete the other pass, i.e. player A a standing pass and player B a dive pass. The receivers return the ball and join the opposite line.

Practice 5

The scrum-half faces a semi-circle of four players numbered one to four. The rugby ball is rolled away and the scrum-half is told the type of pass (dive, pivot, stand) and the number of the receiver (1–4). The scrum-half moves to the ball and executes the required pass, i.e. a dive pass to no. 3 or a pivot pass to no. 1.

TACKLING

Tackling is a very satisfying part of the game and a most important one. Correct technique, paying due regard to safety is very important. Players will soon realise that they will not be hurt and that tackling can be good fun; this will help them to develop confidence in their ability to tackle players from any angle. The coach should constantly remind the players to keep their head behind or to the side of the oncoming attacker. The first point of contact in the tackle should be the *shoulder* immediately followed by the arms acting as a lasso around the legs. By giving the tackled player a ball to hold and a line to score over, the practice immediately becomes more realistic.

Tackling Practice

1. Tackling practices are best done little and often. In a practice session it is better to spend ten minutes on tackling practices repeated two or three times than a twenty-five minute spell trying to show all the tackles likely to be

needed in a game.
2. Give the player to be tackled a ball and a line to score over. This helps to stop the tackled player falling down before the tackle is completed, a common problem with beginners. This also takes away the cold-blooded nature of many tackling practices.
3. Remove boots or allow players to wear training shoes in the early stages.
4. Start beginners on their knees.
5. Progress to walking, jogging and finally running.

The Side Tackle *(Fig 30)*

This is the most common tackle in the game. The tackler tries to force his opponent across the field and drives in to tackle him as he tries to run past.

Checkpoints

1. Drive in low to make shoulder contact with the opponent's thigh, to knock his knees together. The target area is the line of shorts and thigh.
2. Head behind opponent's buttocks.
3. Wrap arms around thighs and pull tight. Hold on.
4. Land on top of opponent.

Practices for the Side Tackle *(Figs 32 & 33)*

Players start on their knees. One player of each pair picks up the rugby ball and dives to score over a try line two to three metres away. As soon as the players touch the ball the tacklers move forward to make their tackle. When competent at this level, the same practice can be repeated from a press-up position or with players on their feet, the ball being placed one metre in front on the floor. The player to be tackled has the incentive of

Fig 29   A well executed front tackle by
          Adam Fox (Harlequins).

Fig 30   Jeremy Guscott (Bath and England)
          making a strong tackle on Harvey
          Thorneycroft (Northampton and England).

31

Fig 31   Harvey Thorneycroft (Northampton)
keeping the ball alive in
spite of Harlequins' pressure.

scoring a try, thus taking his mind off the tackle, whereas the tackler has the objective of completing a successful tackle before his opponent is able to score the try. During the progression the player on his feet has to slow down in order to pick up the ball from the floor, therefore reducing speed and in the early stages making for a safer tackling practice.

The Front Tackle
(Figs 34 & 35)

The same common principles apply as in the side tackle, except that it is important for young players to be discouraged from attempting to crash tackle their opponents by knocking them backwards. The tackler should use the opponent's momentum to complete the tackle.

Checkpoints

1. Drive in low with the shoulder; the target area is the line of shorts and thigh. Keep head to the side of the opponent.

2. Wrap arms around thighs, pull tight and hold on.
3. Allow opponent's momentum to complete the tackle by falling backwards.
4. Turn opponent to finish on top.

Practices for the Front Tackle *(Figs 37 & 38)*

The tackler crouches approximately two or three metres in front of a try line, between the touch-line and the five metre line. The attacker, carrying a ball, walks forward and attempts to score over the try line. As soon as the tackler has completed his tackle and regained a crouching position, the second attacking player walks forward, to be followed by the third player and so on to give a series of perhaps five successive tackles. As the technique improves and the player becomes more confident in his ability, the attacking players should be encouraged to jog forward and then to run more quickly.

*Fig 32   Kneeling side tackle – starting
position.*

*Fig 33   Kneeling side tackle – completed
tackle.*

Fig 34   Tim Rodber (Northampton and England) drives aggressively into the tackle of Neil Matthews (Gloucester and England B).

Fig 35   An aggressive front tackle
executed by Rob MacNaughton of
Northampton.

Fig 36 Ben Clarke (Bath and England) in
a double tackle from Wayne Shelford and
Tim Rodber (Northampton).

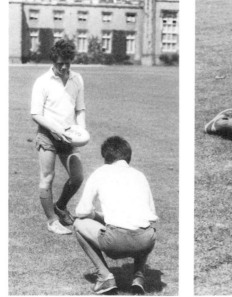

Fig 37 The front tackle – starting position.

Fig 38 The front tackle.

Fig 39   The tackle from behind.

The Tackle from Behind
(Fig 39)

The same basic principles are required to successfully complete the tackle from behind.

Checkpoints

1. Drive low to make shoulder contact with the line of the shorts and thigh, keeping the head to one side.
2. Wrap arms around thighs, pull tight and hold on. As the opponent falls to the ground, try to turn to the side so that tackler's head lands on top.
3. If the opponent is running away from the tackler, it may be necessary to aim slightly higher than the ideal area, then allow the arms to slide down to complete the tackle.

Practices for the Tackle from Behind

The players are positioned one behind the other with the tackler to the rear. On knees initially, the attacking player crawls forward, picks up the rugby ball and attempts to score over the try line approximately five metres in front. The tackler follows behind and executes a rear tackle in order to prevent the score. As the technique improves, allow the players to start on their feet at a walk, a jog and then a run.

Revision of General Principles

1. Incessant emphasis on basic techniques and safety aspects.
2. Careful progression from kneeling to running.
3. Use partners of same size.
4. Practise little and often.
5. Avoid cold-blooded tackling practices. Use a rugby ball and a try line as an incentive for both tackler and tackled player.

KICKING

Kicking is often discouraged with young players. While agreeing that it is important for them to develop their range of handling skills, kicking is an essential part of the game of rugby football and all players, especially threequarters, must develop a repertoire of kicking skills. In the early stages with young players it may be necessary to restrict kicking to either certain players or to certain parts of the field in order to discourage aimless kicking during the game. When one considers the amount of time that players spend kicking a ball around at the start and end of practice sessions, the level of kicking skills shown in matches even at the highest level is very poor. Players should be encouraged to practise kicking with a partner for accuracy, variety and consistency and discouraged from practising faults. A threequarter's repertoire should include the punt, the chip, the grubber kick and the drop kick.

The Punt *(Figs 40 & 41)*

Used as a clearing kick to touch, as a high attacking kick chased by threequarters to pressure the opposition or as a long diagonal kick to gain ground.

Checkpoints

1. Ball should be held at an angle pointing slightly towards the touch-line. For kicks to the left touch-line using the right foot, the right hand should be on top of the ball with the fingers spread. The left hand is placed to the side of the ball with the fingers spread below the ball *(Fig 40)*.
2. Ball is placed along the kicking foot in the same direction as it is being held. It is important that the ball is dropped or placed onto the foot and not thrown into the air – this can change the angle of the ball onto the foot and wastes precious time.
3. The kicking foot swings forward through the ball, body weight moving forward towards the ball to give added power. At the moment

Fig 40   The punt – starting position.

*Fig 41   John Steele (Northampton and
England B) showing good balance and a high
follow through.*

of impact, the kicking foot should be pointed at approximately the same angle as the ball.
4. A good follow-through is essential, the kicking leg is extended with the toe pointing in the direction of the kick *(Fig 41)*.
5. Eyes should be on the ball throughout.

When using the left foot to punt the ball to the right touch-line, reverse all the above coaching points. This method of punting the ball will produce what is known as the *screw kick,* where the ball will be seen to rotate as it flies through the air. In the early stages of learning this technique, it is useful to practise with a partner, initially no more than ten metres apart, trying to effect the technique of placing the ball on the foot and the screw action of the ball, aiming for accuracy in the early stages. When the technique is mastered with either foot, the players can move back a few metres thus increasing the difficulty. Players should be discouraged from trying to kick the ball too hard – additional length comes from the timing of the kick rather than from brute strength.

Players should be encouraged to practise with their weak foot as well as with their favoured one. In the heat of the game it is often impossible to get onto the favourite foot and players should be able to kick with equal facility with either foot.

The Chip Kick *(Fig 42)*

Used to place the ball over the head of an opposing player or threequarter line to be regained by the kicker or another player following up. The aim is to hang the ball in the air to be caught by the following up player on the run.

Checkpoints

1. With the right hand on top of the ball and

the left hand underneath, place the ball sideways across the foot. Swing kicking leg through the ball with toe pointed to follow through after impact. Do not try to kick the ball too hard.
2. Keep eyes on the ball throughout.

Practices for the chip kick can take the form of relays, or chipping the ball over the crossbar or opponent's head, the ball to be caught before it touches the ground, or in a two versus one practice with one player aiming to chip the ball over the head of the opponent to be caught by the team-mate following up.

Grubber Kick *(Fig 43)*

This is used to put the ball behind a quickly advancing defence to be regained by the

Fig 42   Ball position for the chip kick.

kicker or another player following up. It could also be used as a kick to touch outside the 22 metre area.

Checkpoints

1. Left hand placed on top of the ball, right hand below, and the ball should be held sideways.
2. Ball is dropped beside the non-kicking foot and as it touches the floor, kicking foot swings through to push the ball forward along the ground. The impact is made with the instep of the kicking foot.
3. Head over the ball and eyes on the ball throughout.

Using this method, accuracy rather than length is the main criterion. For greater length the following method may be used:

1. Ball pointing towards the ground with the right hand on top of the ball and the left hand placed to the side.
2. The ball is dropped on to the kicking foot which is also pointing towards the ground.
3. The ball is kicked forward into the ground to roll forward end over end *(Fig 43)*.
4. Head down, eyes on the ball throughout.

The grubber kick may be used in conjunction with either falling on the ball or picking the ball up as in a relay type practice, or can be used in a grid area as a team activity. The idea is for the team in possession to keep the ball by grubber kicking to a team-mate who either falls on the ball or picks the ball up to regain possession. The opposition can win the ball by beating their opponents to the pick-up or fall and then keep possession by grubber kicking the ball from one player to another. This combines several practices into a small area and is a very useful exercise.

The Drop Kick

This is used to restart the game from the 22 metre line or from the half-way line after an unsuccessful conversion attempt. It may also be used to score three points by successfully drop kicking a ball between the posts.

Checkpoints

1. The ball is held with two hands pointing towards the ground.
2. Take one step forward, drop the ball to land on its point opposite the non-kicking foot. As the ball is dropped, the kicking foot swings through to make contact with the ball as it touches the ground *(Fig 44)*.
3. Kicking foot is pointed, impact is made with the laces of the boot. A high follow through is important to lift the ball into the air.
4. Head over the ball and eyes on the ball throughout.

RUNNING

One of the great attractions of the game of rugby football is to see flowing running and handling movements, and especially the player with the ability to take on opposing defences with the side-step or swerve executed at speed. While these attributes are undoubtedly inbred, it is possible with practice to improve a player's ability to take on and beat his opposite number. In the early stages with young players, a game of tag in a grid with lots of players in a small space will reveal to the coach the player with the natural side-step or swerve, who could then be used to demonstrate his technique to other players.

The Side-step *(Fig 44)*

This is the ability to wrong-foot defenders with

Basic Skills

a sudden change of direction executed at speed.

Checkpoints

1. The attacking player runs forward at speed. As the opponent approaches, the attacking player stamps down on his outside foot and pushes off in the opposite direction to pass inside the defender.

2. The attacker must disguise his intentions for as long as possible in order to outwit the opponent. At the moment of executing the side-step the attacking player must drive aggressively inside his opponent.

3. If the attacking player runs at speed, the

Fig 43   Ian Hunter (Northampton and England) demonstrating the rolling grubber kick.

covering defender must also run quickly therefore making it more difficult for him to change direction.

Practices for the Side-step

Attacking players should be positioned midway across the grid carrying a rugby ball. The defenders start in one corner of the grid *(Fig 45)*.

The attacking player's aim is to score a try at the far end of the grid; this will encourage the players to run quickly. The position of the defenders can be varied to start at points no. 2 or 3, also the time of the defenders setting off should be varied so that the attackers will be

Fig 44   Matthew Dawson (Northampton and England) showing superb balance while executing a side-step.

Basic Skills

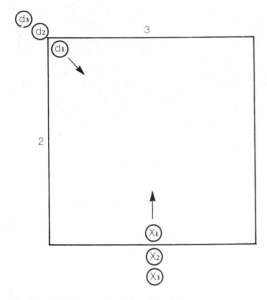

Fig 45 *Starting positions for side-step practice.*

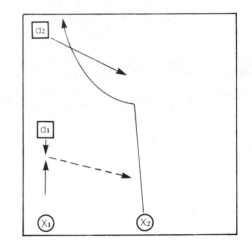

Fig 47 *Two against two side-step game.*

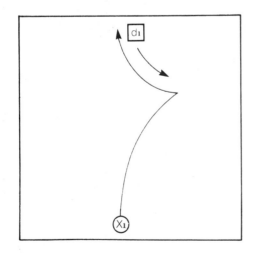

Fig 46 *Side-stepping a defender from the front.*

confronted with a different defensive problem each time. When the defender starts in position no. 3 it will be necessary for the attacking player to run slightly to one side in order to pull the defender out of position before completing the side-step as in *Fig 46.*

This can be developed into a two versus two game, starting positions as in *Fig 47.* Attacker X_1 picks up the ball from in front of him, and as soon as he touches the ball defender d_1 can move forward to defend. X_1 commits the defender and passes to X_2; as soon as X_2 receives the pass, defender d_2 moves forward to defend. Attacker X_2 completes the side-step to score. As the players become proficient in this activity, encourage support from attacker X_1 but always make the second attacker attempt to beat his man with a side-step before looking for the supporting attacking player. Added pressure can then be brought by allowing the defender d_1 to defend twice.

Figs 48 and 49   Ian Hunter using an outside swerve to beat his opponent.

The Swerve *(Figs 48 & 49)*

When a defender is not close enough for the side-step, or the attacking player has more space on his outside, the outside swerve with a change of pace may be used to try to beat the defending player.

Checkpoints

1. The attacker initially runs slightly towards his opponent (feints to turn infield) in order firstly to check the speed of the defender and secondly to keep as much space as possible on his outside.
2. When the defender checks his speed, the attacking player accelerates in an arc away from him; his hips will move slightly away from the defender making the tackle more difficult. The ball should be transferred to the outside arm during this manoeuvre as this allows the hand-off.

Practices for the Swerve

Practices used for the side-step can be adapted for the swerve, although it will be necessary for the defenders always to approach from the side and not to stand in front. By varying the position of the defender, it will then be possible to develop a combination of side-step and swerve. The attacking player has to make note of the position of the defender and then beat him with a side-step or swerve as required.

Running skills are a vital part of the game. Young players should be encouraged to take on their opposite numbers in one versus one, two versus two situations. Players will never develop confidence if the ball carrier continually kicks in these situations as so often happens. Pass and support should be the rule so that if the attempt to beat the defender is unsuccessful, the ball can be kept alive by a pass to supporting players.

SUMMARY

I cannot emphasize enough the importance of basic skills in the game of Rugby Football. Coaches should spend time during each session on a variety of skills. This may be part of the warm up with all players, or could be integrated into the unit skills work, where time could be given to individuals.

1. Handling skills are the bread and butter of *all* rugby players, so emphasize the basics: receiver to present a target, passer to give a sympathetic pass into the target area.
2. Gradually widen the players' repertoire of passes, to enable them to cope with a variety of situations in the field of play.
3. Remember to build confidence when introducing tackling skills, by removing the cold-blooded nature of many practices – give the tackled player a ball and a line to score over. More injuries occur in the tackle than any other phase of the game so emphasize the position of the head – out of danger.
4. Make kicking practices realistic, kicking for accuracy and to develop a range of kicking skills.
5. Running with the ball is what the game is all about. Develop variations in pace and direction to beat a defender.

3 Building Forward Skills

APPROACH

Rugby teams at all levels spend a great deal of time on the various aspects of forward play. It is very rare for a successful team to have a poor pack, but we often see dominant forwards on the losing side. It is possible for forwards to dominate and yet provide poor ball for the backs. It is important therefore to relate forward play to the team requirements – well controlled slow ball is of little value to a threequarter line with the opposing team lining up to tackle. How often do we see the ball held by the No. 8 in a scrummage with the pack attempting to push their opponents backwards before the scrum-half is presented with the ball – and quite often the opposition back row as well! The ball is often tapped from a line-out to another forward who holds the ball while a maul is formed around him, allowing the opposition backs to move up to the new offside line, thus depriving the side in possession of time and space. The emphasis in broken play has been on mauls rather than the quicker ball produced from the ruck, causing yet another problem for threequarters. The simple rule should be to produce the ball while still moving forward; static ball is of little value to the team. Variety is also important – the ball may be held occasionally, it may be driven forward, but the production of quick ball must be a priority.

General Skills for Forwards

While much of the time spent with the forwards will be on aspects of unit play – scrummaging, line-out, rucking and mauling, I think it is important that some time is spent developing the individual skills of the players.

Handling

The ability to regain possession of the ball knocked to the floor is a very important one with forwards. The following practices will be of value:

Scoop and Pass

Players line up in single file in small groups on the goal-line with the ball approximately five metres in front of them on the floor. The first player runs out, scoops the ball up with one hand and runs forward with the ball balanced overhead, turns and replaces the ball ready for the next player. This should be repeated with both the right and the left hand. When players have mastered this, the next stage is to scoop the ball from one hand into the next so that the ball is quickly under control, and then to pass the ball to a supporting player. If the ball is scooped with the right hand under the ball, it is passed to a player supporting on the left and vice versa. The player receiving the pass then puts the ball down on the floor ready for the same pair to repeat the exercise on their return.

Controlling a Rolling Ball

Each player in turn rolls the ball forward, runs after it, stamps one foot beyond the ball to stop the forward movement of the ball, picks the ball up in two hands and passes it back to a team-mate. The object is to control the

Fig 50 Controlling and feeding a rolling ball.

Fig 51 Feeding a ball under pressure.

movement of the ball before it is picked up. The development of this is for the player to roll the ball forward, fall on the ball to control it, the next player places his foot beyond the fallen player and the ball, and passes the ball to a running player in support who places the ball on the ground for the exercise to continue (Fig 50). When the players are proficient in this exercise the pressure can be increased by adding a defender or two (Fig 51). The ball is placed on the floor, a player runs out and falls on the ball. As soon as he touches the ball a team-mate and a defender run forward. The team-mate tries to step beyond the ball as practised previously, secure the ball in his hands and pass it to a supporting runner. The defender runs around a cone and tries to prevent the pass.

Passing

Already covered in Chapter 1 are the screen pass and the maul pass which are very important weapons in the armoury of the forwards. I would like to develop these and put them under more pressure, working initially in small groups with one player standing no more than five metres in front of the group acting as a defender, and at all times attempting a holding tackle (i.e. attempting to stop the forward movement of the ball carrier but not put him on the floor).

In the first exercise the ball carrier drives into the defender with a good driving body position leading with the shoulder, driving the defender backwards, and presents a short screen pass to the supporting player. The ball carrier is attempting on contact to unbalance the defender thus making it more difficult for the defending player to move on to tackle the receiver of the pass.

Assuming that the ball carrier is unable to make a pass, his arms being trapped by the defending player, it is therefore necessary for the next player arriving to get his hands onto the ball. We are now in the very early stages of setting up a maul. What should happen at this stage is that both players continue driving forward with the ball in their possession. The second player will drive forward into the space beyond the defender, the first player will try to free himself and roll around the defender and thus both players are attempting to run into the open, still in possession of the ball. It is very important that the players lead with opposite shoulders, in other words the ball carrier is leading with his right shoulder, the next player leads with his left, thus presenting a screen on either side of the ball. Numbers can be increased as the skill level improves so we could have three players attacking against two defenders, four attacking against three ánd so on, always weighted in favour of the attacking side in the early stages. The object at all times is to free at least one player with the ball in his possession. It is important to keep emphasising that the players are driving forward, keeping the ball away from the defending side. This forward movement makes it difficult for the defending side to organise themselves in such a way as to prevent it and gain possession of the ball.

CONTACT

As part of a warm-up or in the early stages of coaching forwards, it is important that some contact activity takes place in order to strengthen the players and harden them up for the sort of knocks and bangs which are an everyday part of a forward's game.

Crouch and Barge

Players in pairs or threes in a crouching position with their arms folded across their chest. Bouncing on two feet from this position the players barge into each other, shoulder to shoulder, attempting to knock each other to the floor. It is important to encourage the use of both shoulders, not just the dominant arm.

Shoulder Barging

Players in a standing position step forward and make contact, first with the right shoulder, step back, step forward again and make contact with the left shoulder, step back and again with the right shoulder and so on. The players attempt to establish a rhythm whereby they can bounce, step, bounce, step. Again the arms should be folded across the chest in the early stages.

Jump and Barge

This time the players jump into the air and make shoulder contact. This will help to establish balance in the air and balance on landing. Initially, the arms should be folded across the chest prior to contact, but as the players become more confident and proficient in finding their balance, they may be allowed to stretch for an imaginary rugby ball and make contact with the arms outstretched above their heads.

Falling and Rolling

There are a number of ways in which contact with the ground can be introduced, carrying a rugby ball, completing a forward roll and leaving the ball behind, falling on the ball, rolling to the feet and so on. When these things have been completed and again the players are competent at controlling their body weight on contact with the ground, the pressure can be increased by completing the same exercise over a crouched body. The players arrange themselves in a circle with enough distance between each player for a roll to be completed. Players will initially be on their hands and knees. Each player in turn dives over the back of the crouching player, completes a forward roll and continues on to the next player until he arrives back at his place in the circle. The players follow each other around the circle.

SCRUMMAGING

The scrummage is a most important phase of the game of rugby football. It is one area of the game where a team can be reasonably assured of retaining possession of the ball. A well organised side should be able to ensure that on their put-in, the ball is won in a well controlled manner. Once again I think it is important that a great deal of work is carried out with young players on strengthening and technique work prior to any scrummaging session. This is particularly important for players new to the game or at the beginning of a school term or a new rugby season. Young players need a great deal of strengthening work of the shoulder joint, shoulder girdle and neck area, and a great deal of technique work prior to being submitted to the full eight-man scrummage.

Strengthening Activities

Exercise 1 (Fig 52)

One versus one on hands and knees in a scrummaging position. From this basic starting position, a number of strengthening exercises can be undertaken. One player attempts to lift the other by using his head only; the second player is trying to push down with his shoulder in order to prevent himself from being lifted off the ground. Players should take turns in lifting and pressing down and should use both their right and left shoulders. Secondly, the players push sideways against their partners' heads trying to push the head out of the side of their one versus one scrummage. Finally, the players can actually attempt to push each other backwards from this scrummaging position on hands and knees.

Exercise 2

From a standing position, both players place one hand on their opponent's forehead and attempt to push their partner backwards. It is important that the players keep their head up and their neck rigid; the object is to strengthen the neck. This exercise can also be undertaken with a hopping action, each player standing on one leg and hopping forward attempting to push his partner backwards.

Exercise 3

One versus one with the players getting down into a more orthodox scrummaging position with their heads interlocked, binding on each other. One player is attempting to drive forward to push his partner backwards, the second player is adopting a locked position in order to try to avoid being moved. Both players should ensure that their backs are straight and their heads are up. If the coach stresses the need for the players to push their hips down towards the ground and lift their chin, this will help to keep their backs straight. In the locked position the player will splay his feet slightly trying to make maximum stud contact with the ground and his legs will be locked solid *(Fig 53)*. He is then forming a straight body position from his feet through to his shoulders. The player who is driving will bend his knees, drop his hips and try to drive his partner upwards and backwards. It is important that players undertake this exercise with opponents of a similar size and strength and

that they take turns in practising the techniques of driving and locking out.

Exercise 4

Two versus two lock and drive. The same principles apply as in the previous exercise, except that the players are now binding together around the body in pairs. It is very important to stress at all times during these scrummaging exercises, even in the introductory stages, that the players on no account allow their shoulders to drop below their hips. They should be encouraged to drive forward and upwards, not forward and down towards the ground. The RFU have produced some excellent pamphlets on safety and strengthening exercises and it is recommended that coaches and teachers obtain copies of these and make use of the exercises shown therein.

The Front Row

The front row provides the solid base of the scrummage, the platform upon which the players behind them can transmit their for-

Fig 52   Introducing scrummaging on hands and knees. Note straight backs and shoulders higher than hips.

Fig 53 One against one scrummage – player on the left showing a good locked position.

ward shove into the opposing scrummage. It is important therefore that the front row forwards are technically competent, strong, and able to perform as one unit. The binding and foot positions of the front row are shown in *Fig 54*. The normal binding position is for the hooker to bind over the shoulders of his props and obtain a good strong hold upon the shirt of his props underneath the armpits. The prop forwards will take up a binding position on the waistband of the hooker's shorts, the loose-head prop (left) will adopt a wide foot position – his inside or right foot will be back and across allowing room for the hooker to strike for the ball and his left foot will be slightly forward. He is thus providing a large tunnel through which the hooker will strike the ball.

The tight-head prop again will adopt a wide stance, with his outside or right foot slightly further forward than his left, but there is no need for his legs to be as far apart as the loose-head prop. The hooker should be situated comfortably in between his two prop forwards. The front row will bind tight across the shoulders with plenty of room at hip level

to allow the hooker to move across towards the ball and strike it quickly between the loose-head's feet. The front row should get their feet in position early so that on making contact with their opposite numbers they do not need to move their feet positions at all. The action of shuffling the feet around will unbalance the rest of the scrummage thus making a compact unit more difficult to achieve.

It is important that the hooker spends a great deal of time practising his timing of the strike with his scrum-half. This can be done with the full front row of three against a scrummage machine or with the hooker himself isolated against a goal post or a scrummage machine *(Fig 55)*. It is important to stress yet again that the forwards should at all times keep their heads up and their backs straight, and should never allow their shoulders to drop below their hips.

The Lock Forwards

The two locks provide most of the forward

Fig 54   The front row binding and foot positions.

Fig 55   Hooker and scrum-half practice.

drive in a scrummage. It is important that they work together in trying to provide maximum amount of forward momentum. The locks bind together tightly on the waistband of their partner's shorts; dropping down on the inside knee, they will then bind on the front row in one of two ways. In the early stages, with young players I think it is safer for them to take an outside bind around the hips of their prop forwards (Fig 56). As the players increase in

Building Forward Skills

Fig 56   Lock forwards binding round props' hips.

studs on the ground. Lock forwards should be adept at pushing forward from this position, dropping the hips, bending the knees, tightening the arms and then straightening everything as the ball comes in. They must be able to hold a good strong locked position to withstand the expected shove from their opponents as their own scrum-half puts the ball into the scrum.

The No. 8

The No. 8 is the anchor of the scrummage, providing stability and controlling the ball for the scrum-half to feed to his threequarters. The No. 8 will bind around the hips of his lock forwards, his legs back, again obtaining maximum purchase from the ground from a splayed feet position, knees slightly bent, hips down, arms tight ready to give a forward surge as the ball comes into the scrummage, and head up looking at the ball. A tight bind on the lock forwards is essential in order to give them added stability.

Flankers

The flankers will give balance to the scrummage but have a very important scrummaging role in helping their prop forwards by preventing their hips from moving sideways out of the scrummage. The flanker scrummages with his inside shoulder against the buttock of the prop and binds on the lock forward *(Fig 58)*. The left-hand flanker has an important role in controlling the ball as it appears through the legs of the loose head prop, either slowing it for the scrum-half if more control is wanted through channel one, or redirecting it across to the lock forwards for a channel two or three ball. For a scrummage to be most effective it is essential that the unit works as one. It is not an occasion for players to take a rest. One player not scrummaging to his maximum will have an

strength and technical competence, then they may progress to the binding position normally seen in senior rugby which is through the legs of the prop forward *(Fig 57)* grasping the waistband of the props' shorts. From this kneeling position, once they have obtained a strong grip on their prop forward, they move up into their pushing position. It is important that they have their legs back and feet splayed in order to get maximum purchase from their

Fig 57   Lock forwards binding through props'
          legs.

Fig 58   The formation of the scrummage.

adverse effect on the unit as a whole. The other seven players must do all they can to ensure that the hooker has every opportunity of striking cleanly for the ball. The forwards must be encouraged to adopt a positive attitude to their scrummaging.

Checkpoints

1. Shoulders above hips at all times, straight back.
2. Front row provides a solid base for the scrummage.
3. The other seven players are working to give the hooker the best chance of winning the ball.
4. Drop hips and tighten the arms immediately prior to the put-in.
5. Straighten legs and hold the locked posi-

tion as the ball comes in.
6. All eight players *must* work together to produce a successful scrummage.

Channelling the Ball *(Fig 60)*

It is important for the forwards to appreciate the difference in the way the ball is presented to the scrum-half. A small light pack of forwards who may be under pressure in the scrummage will need to be adept at striking the ball and clearing it from the scrummage quickly before the opposition has the opportunity to exploit their physical advantages – a channel one heel would therefore be appropriate. As the players become stronger and technically more proficient, a channel two or three heel will give them more control and more options at the base of the scrum.

Fig 59   A well-formed scrum in this match between the North Midlands and Lancashire.

Channel One

This is where the ball is struck very quickly by the hooker through the tunnel between the loose-head's legs and directly out of the scrummage between the left-hand flanker and the left-hand lock. This clears the ball from the scrummage extremely quickly but does put pressure on the scrum-half to move the ball away quickly. It is difficult for the scrum-half to do anything other than produce a very quick pass to his outside-half. Channel one ball is very useful when the scrummage is under pressure or when the threequarters require quick ball in attack.

Channel Two

A channel two ball is controlled by the left-hand lock forward before being presented to the left-hand side of the No. 8. The ball will come back more slowly through the scrummage therefore allowing the scrum-half more time in which to pass the ball to his three-quarters. It may be necessary during a channel two heel for the left flanker to control a very quick heel and redirect it via the left-hand lock to the feet of the No. 8.

Channel Three

For a scrummage which is technically competent and physically strong, a channel three heel will give the scrum-half the maximum amount of time and protection and allows a variety of options to be played from the base of the scrummage. The ball is struck as for channel two but it is redirected via the left-

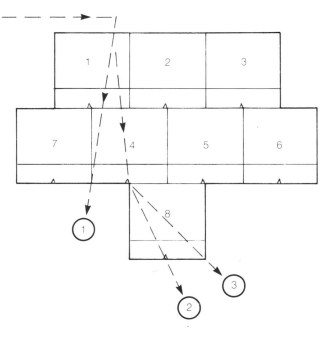

Fig 60 The scrum; channels one, two and three.

Fig 61   Wayne Shelford (Northampton and New Zealand) looking for communication from his scrum-half.

hand lock to the right-hand side of the No. 8's feet. The scrum-half will then have the body of his left-hand flanker and No. 8 protecting him from the opposition scrum-half. It is from a channel three ball that the scrum-half has most options and back row moves will work most effectively. In the early stages of learning scrummaging channel one or two should be sufficient for young players to master. As they become stronger and more experienced in the game, the channel three ball will give far more variety to their game. I think it is important that the players use all three channels during the course of a game except in exceptional circumstances and not get carried away with trying to produce a channel three ball throughout the game. Slow ball is of little benefit to the threequarters – variety and control are important in channelling the ball.

Back Row In Attack

Once the forwards are competent in their scrummaging technique and can channel the ball with good control through channels one, two and three, it is possible to add variety to the team's attack by launching the back row at the opposition. In order to obtain quicker ball the No. 8 may move into the channel one hole, ie. he packs between the left-hand lock and left-hand flanker.

No. 8 Pick-up and Drive (Fig 61)

1. The ball is heeled quickly to the feet of the No. 8.
2. The No. 8 detaches from the scrummage, picks up the ball and drives to his right.
3. *He then has to make a decision (a)* to drive on himself, *(b)* commit the opposition and

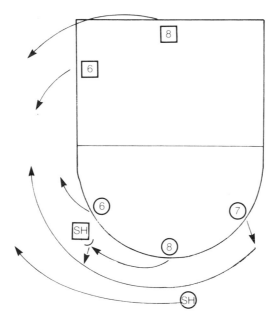

Fig 62   Breaking flanker back row move.

pass to the scrum-half on his outside, or *(c)* commit the opposition and pass the ball to the supporting flanker on his inside.

4. The object of the move is to commit the opposition back row to tackle and to set one attacking player free with support, or to engage the opposition back row in a ruck or maul before presenting the ball to the three-quarters to attack.

Breaking Flanker (Fig 62)

1. A quick heel to the feet of the No. 8.
2. The right-hand flanker breaks behind the back foot of the scrummage. He can only break when the ball is in front of him except in the wheel otherwise he is in an offside position.
3. The No. 8 picks up the ball with his back to the opposition and feeds a short pass to the flanker who drives up the left-hand side of the scrummage. If the No. 8 is under pressure from the opposing scrum-half or

flanker it may be necessary to keep the ball close with the flanker driving into his No. 8 and taking a close screen pass.

4. *He then has to make a decision (a)* to drive on himself, or *(b)* commit the opposition and feed the ball to the left-hand flanker, the No. 8 or the scrum-half who are running in support.
5. The object is to set a man running free in open play or to commit the opposition back row before releasing the ball to the three-quarters.

Back Row In Defence

The back row have an important role to play in the organisation of a team's defence, either as prime defenders close to the set pieces or working with the threequarter line to pressurise the opposition when possession is lost. The three members of the back row must work together as a unit and must be fully conversant with the roles of the other players.

Building Forward Skills

From a Scrum (Fig 63)

The *open side flanker* will initially cover any break by the opposing scrum-half or back row to his side of the scrum. As soon as the ball is passed by the scrum-half, the open side flanker follows as quickly as possible, trying to tackle the outside-half and then exerting pressure on each player as the ball is moved along the threequarter line. The open side flanker's aim is to take man and ball if possible, and to support his own threequarter line if they tackle their opposite numbers by attempting to regain possession of the ball.

The *No. 8* will break from the scrum and follow the open side flanker across the field. He will cover any break on the inside of the flanker, for example a switch move, and moves in quickly to give the flanker support at the breakdown.

The *blind side flanker* must initially make sure that no move is coming around his side of the scrum. As the ball is moved to the opposition outside-half, his task is to cover behind his open side and No. 8 forward giving depth to the defence, covering for any breaks by the opposing threequarters or kicks ahead.

From a Line-out (Fig 64)

The end man in the line-out, usually the *open side flanker,* should, where possible, not get involved in the line-out or the ruck or maul which may be formed. Once again his job is to pressurise the opposing outside-half as he gets the ball. From a line-out the flanker will be ten metres closer to the opposing backs than his own outside-half, and therefore much more likely to force a mistake. If the opposition attempt a peel around the tail of the line-out,

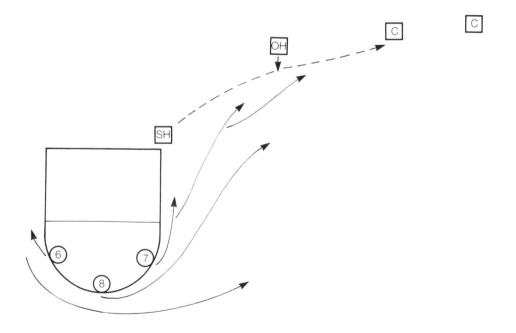

Fig 63   Back row defence from scrums.

the flanker is responsible for the first man.

The *No. 8* may attempt to move through the line-out to pressurise the opposing scrum-half; the hooker from the front forms the other arm of the pincer. As the ball is moved to the threequarters, the No. 8 covers on the inside of the flanker as from a scrum. The No. 8 must contest any ball thrown to the back of the line-out.

The *blind side flanker* has an important role as supporting player to his own jumper at No. 4 in the line-out. This initial job will tie him to the line-out for longer than the two players behind him: this means that his line of running in defence is again much deeper, giving him a covering role.

Practices for the Back Row

The aims are to improve speed off the mark and competition for the ball on the floor.

Exercise 1

A back row forward in a scrummage position against each of the uprights. The coach, standing between the posts, rolls a rugby ball forward and on the command the players race to fall on the ball. Each player is aiming to put his body between the ball and his opponent.

Exercise 2

Two players (No. 8 and flanker) against each post as in Exercise 1. The flankers compete for the ball on the floor (stationary or rolling) supported by the No. 8. The flanker may be able to pass the ball to the No. 8 or merely roll the ball back to the supporting player. The third member to each back row may then be added.

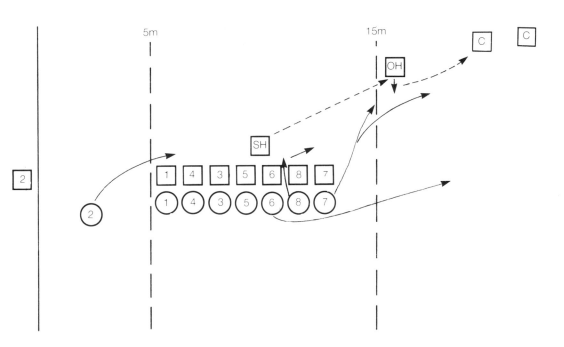

Fig 64   Back row defence from the line-out.

Building Forward Skills

Exercise 3

Rugby ball placed on top of a tackle bag ten metres out from the goal-posts. The three members of the back row adopt a scrummage formation by one goal-post. On the command, the nearest flanker tackles the bag thus freeing the rugby ball for the No. 8 and blind side flanker to use in attacking the 22 metre line. A scrum-half and threequarter line may be added to this practice.

THE LINE-OUT

In the line-out as in the scrummage it is essential that all players work together in order to ensure possession of the ball. The most important people are the thrower and the jumper. They must work closely together in order to perfect the timing and accuracy of their throwing and jumping, but it is equally important that the supporting players should know their roles in order to obtain tidy possession for the scrum-half.

Individual Skills

The thrower must be able consistently to put the ball into the place specified by his jumper, be it a hard flat throw to a front jumper, or a lobbed throw to the middle or back of the line-out. He should therefore be able to change the trajectory and speed of his throw as indicated by the jumper concerned. The thrower can practise on his own with a hoop suspended from a post or crossbar of the goal-posts or marks against a wall at varying heights.

The jumpers should measure the height that they can jump with an outstretched hand and with exercises such as squat jumps or step-ups, attempt to increase the height which can be reached over the course of a

season.

A useful repetitive exercise with a ball is for the jumper to be faced by two or three other players each in possession of a rugby ball. Each player in turn lobs the ball into the air above the head of the jumper who jumps up, catches it and returns the ball whilst still in the air. As soon as his feet touch the ground, the second player will throw his ball into the air for the player to catch and return and again this will be repeated with the third player. The aim is for the player to control the ball while in mid-air, but the repetitive nature of the practice should increase his vertical jump. Variations can be introduced in that the ball may be caught and returned or may be palmed directly back to the person who has thrown the ball to the jumper. An opposing player may be introduced so that every time the jumper touches the ball in mid-air, the opposition gives him a slight nudge or push so that he has to resist the pressure of the opposition and still control the ball. Volleying practices are also useful, helping the big forwards to maintain control of the ball with their hands in the air. Four or five players together in a circle will attempt to keep the ball in the air for as long as possible by playing it with one or two hands to the players alongside them.

Throwing In

As has been stressed already, it is very important that the person throwing the ball into the line-out can repeat consistently the type of throw required by his jumpers. In the early stages with very young players it may be necessary to revert to the two-handed underarm throw which was widely used in the game a few years ago. A young player will find difficulty in throwing the ball accurately over any great distance and this may be one method of successfully getting the ball to a jumper near the front of the line-out. A

Fig 65   Hooker John Olver (Northampton
and England) finds his man in the
Pilkington Cup Final at Twickenham.

problem arises with the players to the middle and tail of the line-out in that they cannot see the ball until much later in its flight as it will be blocked by the players standing in front of them. Nevertheless I would not discourage this type of throw in the early stages of line-out play.

Two-handed Overhead Throw

A better method for beginners may be to use a soccer type, two-handed overhead throw-in. Using this method the ball can be seen from the time it leaves the thrower's hands, thus making the timing of the jump much easier. The problem with this throw is that it is difficult to bring in the variations mentioned already, particularly the flat hard throw.

Torpedo Throw (Fig 66)

This has become the most common type of throw used in the modern game and young players should be encouraged to experiment with this as soon as they are able to control the ball.

The ball is held initially in two hands, just in front of the forehead, the right-handed thrower having his left leg slightly in front of his right. The thrower's eyes will be fixed on their target through the delivery. The right hand is brought back overhead with the ball balanced in the palm of the hands, fingers spread behind the ball (Fig 66). The back will be arched slightly to add impetus to the throw: as soon as the arm reaches its furthest point backwards the jumper will be ready to begin his jump for the ball. The weight is then transferred from the back foot to the front foot, the back is straightened and the throwing arm extended towards the target area. As the ball leaves the hands, the fingers roll across the surface of the ball imparting a torpedo-type spin. Using this basic type method it is possible to produce a variety of throws, according to where in the line-out the ball is to be thrown and the type of throw desired by the jumper on any particular occasion.

Fig 66 A good example of a hooker preparing to throw into a line-out.

Fig 67   John Etheridge (Northampton)
taking the ball at the front of a line-out.

*Fig 68   Martin Bayfield showing good
technique at the front of the line–out . . .*

Fig 69   . . . and in the middle.

Building Forward Skills

The Thrower and Jumper
(Figs 68 & 69)

For a line-out to be successful, the thrower and the jumper must spend a great deal of time perfecting their timing and variations in order that they can be perfectly reproduced in a game situation. In the early stages the thrower and jumper would work with a scrum-half – the object of this exercise being to experiment with differing types of throw. The most important ones for use in a match would be either to step forward and slightly to the middle of the line-out in order to take a hard flat throw, particularly useful for the front jumper *(Fig 68)*, or to feint forward and step backwards to take the high lobbed throw which would be more used in the middle and back of a line-out *(Fig 69)*. The jumper would attempt to catch the ball, turn in mid-air so that he lands with his back to the opposition before feeding the ball to the scrum-half. The jumpers would then practise a deflection direct from the line-out to the scrum-half with two hands and with one hand. When the thrower and jumper are reasonably proficient at their variations and signals, it is then important to add some opposition; initially the opposing player would not compete for the ball in the air but would attempt to bump or push the jumper as he was catching or deflecting the ball. The jumper is thus learning to take some physical contact and still control the ball. The next stage is for the two jumpers to actually compete for the ball so that the success of the timing of the throw with the hooker would be put to a more realistic test.

Role of Supporting Players
(Figs 70 to 73)

For any line-out to be successful, all members of the line-out must know their job so that they can provide maximum support to the jumper

and protection for the scrum-half. This can be built up slowly in the early stages until all the players are competent in their roles. With the formation that we have used in the last exercise, i.e. a thrower, a jumper with opposition and a scrum-half, it would then be necessary to add a supporting player on either side of one of the jumpers. As the jumper leaps into the air and makes contact with the ball, the two supporting players with their faces towards the opposition, step towards the jumper and bind around his waist in order to protect the ball from the arms and bodies of the opposition *(Fig 70)*. As explained earlier, the jumper will turn in mid-air so that a shield around the ball will be provided by the jumper and his immediate supporting players. Additional players can be added and their role is to bind on to the nearest supporting player, thus

Fig 70   Protecting the line-out jumper.

Fig 71   A two-handed catch · ·

adding further protection to the ball and to their scrum-half. The thrower-in will follow the ball after it has left his hand and will add support as necessary at the front of the line-out. The opposition at this stage are being asked to try to get their hands on the ball if possible or to find their way through the line-out to make contact with the scrum-half, thus testing the reactions of the supporting players. Throughout these practices the jumpers should be encouraged to use the variations practised previously, i.e. to catch the ball, to deflect it with one hand or two hands thus making it difficult for the opposition to know exactly when the ball will be released to the scrum-half.

Checkpoints

1. The thrower is the most important man in the line-out – he must *practice* throwing the ball.
2. Thrower and jumpers must constantly practise their timing and variations.
3. Provide quick solid support for the jumper to protect the ball from the opposition.
4. Pressure the opposition on their throw-in.
5. Use variations of two-hand catch or one/two-hand deflection to keep opposition guessing.

Short Line-outs

A side should take onto the field some line-out variations in the form of reduced numbers, i.e. two man or four man line-outs. This is particularly important to combat the side which is physically far superior, therefore dominating the line-out, but also to provide a variety of attack. The forwards not involved directly in the line-out can be used as a launching pad for a concerted drive at the opposing outside-half. I will deal with two variations of a short line-out but there are a number of alternatives which can be used by the thoughtful player and coach.

Fig 72   . . . and feed.

Fig 73   A two-handed deflection giving
quick ball from line-out.

Fig 74   Two-man line-out; variation one.

Variation 1 (Fig 74)

A two man line-out with the two players involved spread approximately five metres apart. The rear player walks backwards followed by his opponent, after either a predetermined number of steps – say, four, or a signal from the thrower, he will move forward to collect the ball leaving his opponent trailing behind him. The jumper will always have the upper hand as he and the thrower will know exactly the timing for the move.

Variation 2

Another two man line-out, but on this occasion both jumpers will move infield followed by their opponents. The ball is thrown into the space created at the front of the line-out and caught by a player running from the scrum-half position. Using the element of surprise, this player should be able to attack, supported by the line-out jumpers and the thrower.

Line-out Peels (Fig 75)

Another useful variation from the line-out is to attack through the forwards, peeling around the end of the line-out in close support. The ball is thrown to the player standing at No. 6 in the line-out, usually the best jumper in the back row, or possibly the middle jumper switched to the tail of the line-out for the purpose of the peel. As the ball arrives, the jumper deflects it to a prop forward running close to the line-out. The end jumper should be encouraged to drop the ball into the path of the peeling player rather than think of tapping the ball away from the line-out. On receiving the ball, the prop forward drives close around the tail of the line-out. *He then makes a decision to (a)* commit the first member of the opposition that he meets, or *(b)* give a short pass to the next supporting player arriving close behind. The suggested order of players for the peel is as follows: first man, prop forward standing at No. 3 in the line-out;

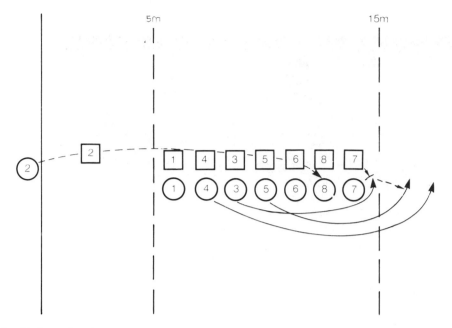

Fig 75   The line-out peel.

secondly the lock forward standing at No. 4; third man, lock forward standing at No. 2. There are no hard and fast rules about this and it may be that other combinations are more suitable to a particular team. All forwards should be alert during the peel, as is the scrum-half, so that a badly deflected ball or one that has been missed by the supporting players can be rescued by either the scrum-half and fed to his threequarters, or by the players following up the initial peeling forward. Teams who are unable to perfect a peel around the tail of a line-out may work on a front peel. The ball would be thrown to No. 2 or No. 3 in the line-out with the peel carried out by Nos 5, 6, and 7 driving up the 5 metre area.

There are other simple line-out variations which may also be considered.

1. Move a jumper to No. 1 in the line-out. This can provide quick ball to the throwing in side, and can also be used as a defensive ploy to prevent an opponent's throw to their front jumper.
2. Doubling up the jumpers. By standing two or more jumpers one behind the other, the throwing in side increases the target area for their thrower and with more than one player jumping it becomes difficult for the opposing side to pick out the ultimate target for the ball. If two jumpers stand at the end of a line it is possible to nullify the effectiveness of the open side flanker. The No. 7 will either move to another position in the line-out to be replaced by one of his side's jumpers, or he will be committed to the line-out by the long throw, thus unable to challenge the opposing outside-half.

RUCK AND MAUL

Having won the ball from the set piece, a team can attack in a variety of ways. The opposition will be doing all they can to stop these attacks and obtain possession of the ball. Therefore, all teams should be well versed in ways of retaining possession of the ball in contact or breakdown situations. All players, whether they are threequarters or forwards, should know their role in both the ruck or the maul.

Fig 76 Forward driving body position.

Speed is of the essence – the side in possession of the ball must get more of their players in support of the ball carrier than the opposition in order to ensure the continuity of the attack.

Ruck *(Figs 76 to 79)*

Definition A ruck is formed when the ball is on the ground and one or more players from each team are on their feet and in physical contact, closing around the ball between them.

Advantages of the Ruck

1. It produces quick ball.
2. It is dynamic, producing the ball while going forward, the opponents being forced to retreat often being disorganised.
3. Each player's role is simple.

The Role of the Ball Carrier

The ball carrier's role in setting up the ruck will vary according to whether he is tackled to the floor by his opponent or whether he is able to remain on his feet, still in possession of the ball. The ball carrier should adopt a low body position leaning forward, leading with his shoulder, driving into the opponent in an attempt to knock them backwards *(Fig 76)*. If he is tackled to the ground he should ensure that he falls with his body between the ball and the tackler to protect the ball from the opponents.

Supporting Players

The supporting players must immediately step beyond the ball and the player on the floor, binding with each other to provide a solid base from which the following players can bind and drive *(Fig 77)*. The next arriving players, binding together, will drive hard and low into those players straddling the ball and drive the whole of the ruck clear of the ball thus leaving the ball for the scrum-half to clear to his threequarters *(Fig 78)*. It is important that all players keep their heads up and use the ball as a target beyond which they will drive, backs

Fig 77 Providing a solid base for the ruck.

Fig 78 The ruck.

should be straight and arms binding firmly on their team-mates to provide a very solid platform. A simple rule for players arriving at the ruck is *bend* (knees) *bind* (on a team-mate) and *drive* (beyond the ball).

Ball Carrier on Feet

If the ball carrier is able to remain on his feet as he drives into the opponent, he should attempt to place the ball between his feet while adopting a forward driving position with his head up and back straight *(Fig 79)*. He thus provides the platform onto which quickly arriving team-mates can bind and drive beyond the ball. The role of the arriving players is the same as for the player tackled to the floor and setting up the ruck. The advantage of the player remaining on his feet is that he provides an immediate platform on which his team-mates can bind and drive. The tendency when the player is tackled to the floor is that the arriving players as they step beyond the ball fall to the floor, thus creating a pile of bodies around the ball.

Checkpoints

1. Shoulders always above hips.
2. Adopt a strong forward driving body position.
3. *Bend* knees, *bind* on team-mate or opposition and *drive* beyond the ball.
4. Be dynamic – drive in hard and low.

Practices for the Ruck

Build the ruck up slowly, stressing continuously the body position of the players.

Exercise 1

This can be carried out across a grid with groups of five players. The pairs bind together facing each other approximately five metres apart with a ball placed behind them. The remaining player will run across the grid driving alternately into first one group and then the other. The supporting players will take the impact with their outside arm and by bending at the waist. The driving player should adopt a good forward lean with his head up and back straight, a wide arm position binding together the two opponents and drive aggressively beyond the ball *(Fig 80)*. The movement of

Fig 79   Good body position in forming the ruck.

Fig 80 *Driving practice for the ruck – head up and back straight.*

Fig 81 *Rucking onto the ball carrier.*

bend, bind and drive should be encouraged throughout.

Exercise 2

Again in groups of five organised as previously but with the driving player in possession of a ball. He drives into the first couple placing the ball on the floor as he makes contact, and drives beyond it. He then turns, picks the ball up and drives into the second pair to be followed by the two who were acting as opposition on the first occasion. The three of them, binding together, will drive into the second couple and beyond the ball; the five players will then turn, the nearest player to the ball picks it up, runs forward five metres, places the ball on the floor and acts as a platform onto which the players can bind and drive beyond the ball *(Fig 81)*. We are thus encouraging close support, the supporting players to bind as they arrive at the ruck and drive beyond the ball.

Exercise 3

Three groups of defenders in pairs are placed approximately ten metres apart along a line. Between each group is situated a cone *(Fig 82)*. The attacking three players will drive into the first couple, picking up the ball as they go along to check their speed; the first player

places the ball on the floor, the two supporting players bind on him and drive beyond the ball. They detach themselves, run around the first cone, pick up the next ball and drive into the facing group of defenders. When they have driven beyond the ball they release the defenders and repeat the exercise around the second cone into the third group of defenders. The rucking players should be encouraged to drive straight forward on each occasion; as they come around the cone they must straighten up and drive parallel. As the groups become more proficient at this exercise numbers may be increased, i.e. five attackers may drive into three or four defenders. The formation of the defending players can be varied, encouraging all the time a change of direction by the rucking players but a drive parallel to what would be the direction of play must be emphasised at all times.

Exercise 4

Five attacking players and three defenders line up on one edge of the grid with a cone placed approximately half-way across the grid area. A ball carrier will move towards the cone and will be tackled by a defender. As soon as the player is tackled the attacking players will move forward, step over him, bind together and ruck over the ball. The defending players will move forward at the same time but have to run around the cone before they can approach the defending player thus giving the attackers time to adopt a ruck formation before they meet the defenders *(Fig 83)*. In the early stages of this practice it may be necessary to send two attackers out slightly ahead of the other three in order that they can provide the platform over the tackled player onto which the other players can bind and drive.

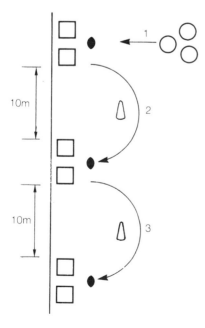

Fig 82 Three against two rucking practice.

Building Forward Skills

Maul *(Figs 84 to 88)*

Definition A maul is formed by one or more players from each team on their feet and in physical contact closing round a player who is carrying the ball.

Advantages of the Maul

1. The ball is controlled.
2. The maul provides time for a defending team to re-group around the ball.
3. The scrum-half dictates when he wants possession of the ball from the maul.

Forming the Maul

1. The ball carrier drives into his opponent with a forward body lean, driving with the shoulder forward. He attempts to unbalance his opponent and adopts a strong position with a wide base, feet spread apart. The ball is pushed towards the nearest supporting player with the body acting as a screen between the ball and the opponent.

2. The first player to arrive drives with the opposite shoulder to the ball carrier to form a triangle with the ball between them thus protecting the ball from their opponents *(Fig 84)*. He puts his hands on the ball but does not take the ball from the initial ball carrier. Thus the ball is protected in a strong position.

3. The next players who should arrive quickly will bind with their inside arm around the outside of the players already forming the wedge. If any opponents are attempting to encroach around the outside of the maul, their outside arm can be used to pull them into the maul. These players are helping to complete the screen and to add forward momentum to the maul *(Fig 85)*.

4. The rest of the pack as they arrive will adopt a low driving position, driving in hard to the maul, equally spaced on either side of the

Fig 83   Five against three rucking practice.

Fig 84   Protecting the ball.

Fig 85   The maul.

Fig 86 *The Saracens' pack illustrating good technique in the maul.*

ball. Players arriving at this stage should not block the movement of the ball to the scrum-half. A common fault is for players to put more and more hands on the ball thus slowing down the transfer of the ball from the maul to the scrum-half. Once the maul has been set up solidly around the ball carrier, there is no need for any more interference with the ball.

Checkpoints

1. Ball carrier adopts a strong driving position protecting the ball with his body.
2. First arriving player leads with *opposite shoulder* and secures the ball.
3. Next players balance the maul on opposite sides of the ball – first man far side, second man near side, etc.
4. Scrum-half decides when he wants possession of the ball.

Practices for the Maul

Exercise 1

Five versus five. The five attacking players will organise themselves as follows: the first, the ball carrier, leading into the first defending player; the second player will drive into the ball carrier and secure possession of the ball; numbers three and four will wedge on either side of the ball, and player five will act as a scrum-half and will receive the feed from the second player. He will then drive into the next defender and take over the role of the ball carrier. The defending players spread themselves approximately five to seven metres apart, slightly offset *(Fig 89)*. The players drive into the first defender, secure the ball, form the wedge and feed to their acting scrum-half who drives into the second defender assisted by the first defender who will loop back to give him some assistance, therefore it becomes five versus two. After securing and winning the

Fig 87   The London Irish scrum-half about
to receive the ball from a maul.

Fig 88   Richard Hill about to pass from the
maul.

Building Forward Skills

ball here, the acting scrum-half, who could be any one of the players at this stage, drives into the third defender assisted by defenders number one and two, and so on into defenders four and five, thus increasing the opposition as the players move from one defender to another. The groups change over so that they are alternately attacking and defending. The sequence of events is *drive* into the defender, *secure the ball, wedge, feed,* and the players should be encouraged to control the ball and not to rush through the exercise thus losing the ball or falling to the ground.

Exercise 2

Using a full pack of eight forwards against opposition groups of five spread at varying positions across the field. The eight players will drive into the opposition, secure the ball, form the wedge around the ball and feed to one of their players who drives into the next group of defending players closely followed by

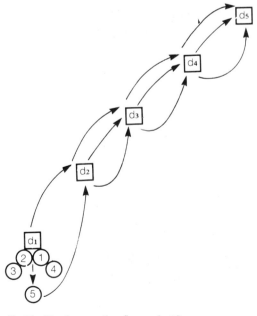

Fig 89   Mauling practice; five against five.

his support. The position of the defenders can be varied in a similar way to that for the ruck exercise shown previously.

Exercise 3 – Ruck versus Maul

With two packs of forwards in a restricted area, i.e. between the touch-line and the 15 metre area. The coach has possession of the ball and moves up and down the touch line; one pack of forwards will be moving forward following him, one pack of forwards retreating. As the coach moves in the opposite direction, the two packs of forwards will change, the side that had previously been going forward retreats and so on. The coach at some stage will give the ball to one side or the other and they react according to their movement, i.e. if they are moving forward, they will be encouraged to form a ruck. If they are moving backwards on receipt of the ball, they will be encouraged to form a maul to re-group round the ball and then counter attack. After a successful ruck or maul has been formed, the ball is returned to the coach who immediately carries on moving in one direction or the other: the players react quickly to his movements and to the ball. This is a very tiring but worthwhile exercise with more experienced players.

Formation of the Maul from a Kick-off

When players are grouped closely round the ball, for example on receiving a kick-off or from a line-out, it is possible to form a maul by a slightly different method. From these two situations, it is guaranteed that the nearest supporting players are very close to the ball catcher therefore offering him immediate protection. In this case the first two players arriving simultaneously should be encouraged to bind on either side of the ball carrier thus offering an immediate protective wedge around the ball *(Fig 90)*. The next arriving players will wedge on either side of the ball balancing up the maul as necessary. A simple rule for players is this: when players are closely grouped around the ball, for example from a kick-off or line-out, they immediately form a wedge on the ball carrier. When the players arrive more slowly, for example from a breakdown in midfield, it will be necessary for the player arriving first to secure possession of the ball as it may be a few seconds before the next player arrives. If the first player leaves the ball and binds around the ball carrier, it may be possible for the opposition still to get their hands on the ball or even to take possession of it. Subsequently arriving players will support alternately on the far side then the near side of the maul giving balance to the maul and protection to the ball carrier.

RUCK/MAUL EXPERIMENTAL VARIATION

The experimental ruck/maul law introduced in season 1992–93 places a greater emphasis on the team in possession of the ball being more constructive with it.

In the 1993–94 season this was again amended as follows: if at a maul the ball becomes unplayable, or the referee decides that the maul has become stationary, a scrum will be awarded with the put in going to the team *not* in possession at the commencement of the maul. The onus is thus on the attacking team to produce the ball quickly or lose possession.

It is vital that the ball is moved quickly to the back of the maul thus ensuring that (i) the opposition cannot get their hands on the ball and (ii) the referee can see that the ball is available. Once a maul stops moving

Fig 90   The maul from a kick-off.

forward the ball must be played immediately as the mauling side are not allowed to start moving again.

Rucking becomes a much safer option

under these new laws because the side going forward into the ruck with the ball will be given the put in at the scrummage should the ball become unplayable.

SUMMARY

Players must improve their strength and technique and develop an awareness of their roles both as an individual player and a member of the unit. Strength work for the front five in particular is an important part of forward preparation: this is particularly so during pre-season training and the early part of the season. Strength work should be relevant to scrummaging and contact. Young players must be given a thorough grounding in the techniques of the scrummage; the body position, the placement of feet, binding and timing of the shove are all important aspects of scrummaging and require constant practice.

1. With young players little and often is the rule: they are not physically able to stand long sessions of intensive work in scrummages. The scrummage is the most reliable source of set-piece possession and teams must be able to capitalise on this aspect of their game.
2. Line-out work should concentrate on the techniques of the individual players, particularly those of the thrower and the catcher. Other players, however, must be aware of their roles in supporting the jumper and tidying up any ball which is knocked away from the line-out, in order to produce quality ball for the threequarters.
3. Players must realise that set-pieces are not an end in themselves but a means of re-starting the game. Having won the ball, they must make the best possible use of it: they must be encouraged to make the *correct decisions* of when to run, when to pass, how and where to support the ball carrier and the timing of the release of the ball to the threequarters.
4. Players should be encouraged to make the most constructive use of the ball. The coach's role is to produce the most efficient unit possible: this will come about by working with the individuals within that unit rather than spending the majority of time on the unit as a whole. Each forward must be encouraged to develop his potential to the full, thereby making a greater impact on the work of the unit.
5. Decision making skills amongst the forwards are most important – how to vary the release of the ball in the scrummage, when to carry out back row moves, the use of the catch or deflection from a line-out in order to unsettle the opposing back row and threequarter line, and how to make best use of the ball when in possession.
6. Finally, forwards should see their role not merely as ball winners but having won possession, must support the ball carrier and become attacking players.

4 The Threequarters

THREEQUARTER SKILLS

The main objective of the threequarters is to make the best possible use of the ball when their side is in possession, if possible to convert this possession into points and at worst to retain possession of the ball when stopped by the opposition. In order to accomplish these tasks it is vitally important that all threequarters are well versed in the individual skills of the game. In this chapter I shall not attempt to run through a number of set moves for the backs. Players should be able to perform the miss pass, the loop, the switch and so on as part of their individual skills training. They should therefore be able to incorporate these into their normal threequarter play. I watch a number of sides that have obviously spent a great deal of time practising complicated set moves only to see such moves break down because of the inability of the players concerned to perform the basic skills under pressure.

Half-backs

These are the linchpin of the side and should provide maximum possible time and space for the players around them to operate. Many teams, even at the highest level, have difficulty in consistently moving the ball along the three-quarter line to the wing. The more time the half-backs need to catch and pass the ball, the more difficult this operation becomes.

The half-backs should consider two aspects of their play and its effects on the people outside of them. Firstly, if the scrum-half passes the ball too far in front of his outside-half, he is encouraging the outside-half to move several paces forward in order to catch the ball; thus he is using up the precious space between himself and the opposing side who are coming forward to tackle him. By doing this he is cutting down the amount of time and space that people on his outside have in which to move the ball. Secondly, if after catching the ball the outside-half runs several paces forward before passing the ball to his centres, the same problem arises – he is cutting down the amount of time and space available for his centres to transfer the ball to the people outside them, thus causing the common problem of players in the middle of the field being caught in possession of the ball. Once the half-backs are aware of these problems, they can look at ways of solving them. I do not advocate the outside-half standing still to catch and pass the ball from scrum and line-out, but I think he should delay his run until the ball is almost in his hands and, having caught the ball, move it within one or two strides.

The scrum-half should be aware of his role in putting the ball in exactly the right place for the outside-half to catch and pass as quickly as possible. Consistency in the scrum-half pass is vital for any threequarter line to move well. The half-backs should spend a great deal of time practising as a pair; they can take a rugby ball to one end of the field, the scrum-half bouncing the ball off the goal posts and then passing to the outside-half who varies his position. The scrum-half is consistently trying to move the ball to where it can be caught and passed within one stride, while reacting to the changing position of his outside-half.

It is then possible to add a defender who comes from the position of the scrum-half acting as a flanker, and also a centre so that the outside-half can move the ball as quickly as possible. The outside-half must vary his position in relation to the scrum-half, sometimes taking a deep pass, or a wider and flatter one, and try to appreciate the problems that this poses for the defending players and the effect it has on the amount of time and room available to those on the outside of him.

The half-backs are thus building a wide repertoire of passes and angles of running which they can bring to use at different phases of the game. By doing this, they are continually posing problems for the defending half-backs and back row. The half-backs should provide a constant threat to the opposition back row thus checking their progress across the field, taking some pressure off the other threequarters. This important but often unnoticed part of the half-backs' play is of great benefit to the other players in the side.

Threequarter Alignments
(Figs 91 to 93)

There is no simple answer to which type of alignment will best suit any given threequarter line; it will depend upon the personnel making up the threequarter line and the phase of the game involved. It may be necessary with younger players for them to stand much deeper than older and more skilful players – certainly players will find that they need to give themselves a little bit more depth from a scrummage where the opposition threequar-

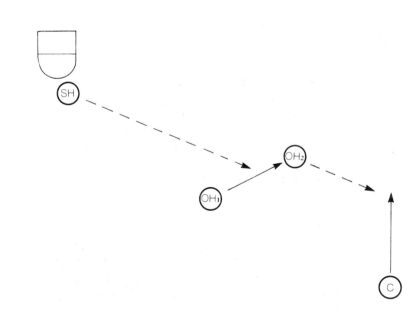

Fig 91   Inside centre's position for outside-half pass.

ters will be much closer than for the line-out. Ruck and maul situations will vary throughout the game and it is up to the attacking three-quarters to align themselves to take the best advantage of what could well be a disorganised defensive alignment. One common fault over the years has been for the threequarters to align much too steeply and to run across the field.

I would like to look at some general principles around which a threequarter line can be adapted. Most outside-halves will tend to move across the field from their starting position to the point where they release the ball to the inside centre. If the inside centre does not take this into account, he will either find himself running too close to his outside-half or being pushed across the field, a situation which must be overcome. I think it is important to position the inside centre relative to the finishing position of the outside-half, i.e. the position from which he passes the ball rather than the position from which he starts his run. This can be done simply by placing a marker on the ground at the outside-half's starting position and one in the position where he passes the ball, and asking the inside centre to adjust his position to the second marker rather than the first. This allows the inside centre to run straighter onto the ball and thus overcome the problem of being pushed sideways by the outside-half. The starting position of the inside centre therefore is two or three yards further across the field than normal. If he starts with the outside foot forward this will also help to encourage a straighter run onto the ball. Encouraging the inside centre to run straighter will have a great effect in combating

Fig 92   Steep alignment, with the inside foot forward, leads to the threequarter line running diagonally across the pitch.

Fig 93   Flatter alignment, with winger in a
wide position, creates space for an
extra man.

the sideways drift of the threequarter line. How deep the inside centre stands in relation to his outside-half depends upon his ability as a catcher and passer of the ball, but as explained earlier he may well need to stand slightly deeper from a scrum ball than from a line-out. The outside centre should take up a position relative to the man inside him which allows him to run straight onto the ball. This may well be a little bit wider than has been normal. Again a starting position with the outside foot forward is important.

It has become the current fashion to launch many threequarter attacks in the area around the outside centre in order to make space for an additional man to enter the threequarter line, usually the full-back, but alternatively the blind-side winger. The open-side winger has been encouraged to adopt a rather wider position than normal. His opposite number will tend to follow him, thus creating space in which to run the extra attacking players (Fig 93). Although starting rather wider than normal, the winger should be encouraged to run slightly in towards his fellow threequarters in order to receive the pass. Again variety is the key word here, the centres and wing should be adept at varying the type of pass and their lines of run, the winger occasionally taking a short pass close to his centre, and then on occasions drifting wide and taking the ball on the outside of his opposite number. The full-back should vary his starting position so as to disguise his intended point of entry into the threequarter line; when he does enter the threequarter line he should inject some pace and if possible change the line of running of the threequarters. On too many occasions the full-back merely becomes a third centre and slows down the progress of the ball to the wing. He must become a prime attacker if he is to enter the threequarter line.

The Gain and Tackle Line
(Figs 94 & 95)

Having established some form of alignment, it is time to introduce the idea of the *gain line* and the *tackle line.*

The Gain Line

The gain line is an imaginary line through the point at which play starts, i.e. middle of scrum or line-out, running parallel to the goal-lines. A team must cross this line in order to gain an advantage from that situation.

The Tackle Line

The tackle line is an imaginary line midway between the two sets of backs. If the three-quarter lines move forward at the same speed, the point at which they meet is the tackle line *(Fig 94).* For any attack to be effective, the team in possession must attempt to push the tackle line over to their opponents' side of the gain line *(Fig 95).* The tackle line pivots in relation to the gain line; the steeper the attacking side stands, the more difficult it will be for them to cross the gain line. The inability of a side to cross the gain line means that the forwards will have to run back from the set pieces in order to support the play.

Practices to Improve the Individual

Players should always be encouraged to pass the ball to the hands of the receiver, not out in front of him encouraging the drift. The receiver puts his hands towards the passer of the ball to take the pass early, moving slightly towards the passer to encourage straight running.

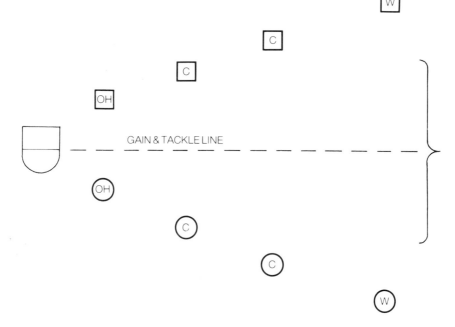

GAIN & TACKLE LINE

Fig 94   The tackle and gain line.

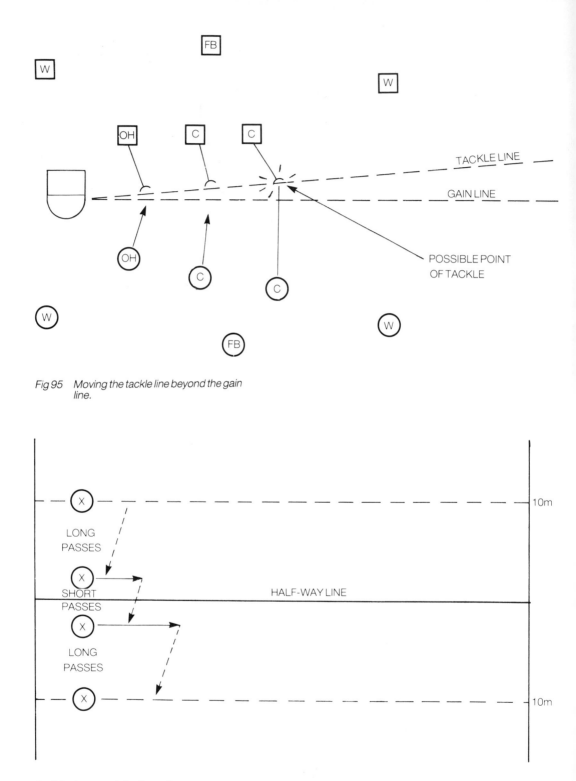

Fig 95   Moving the tackle line beyond the gain
line.

Fig 96   Long and short passing exercise.

Exercise 1 (Fig 96)

In groups of four running across the pitch, vary the length of the passes, long, short, long etc. A useful guide is to have two players side by side running across the half-way line with two players running on each ten metre line. Players must be encouraged to pass the ball to the hands of the receiver.

Exercise 2

In groups of four in the fifteen metre area. The ball is moved along the line to the third player who has to react to the varying position of his wing; the winger will change his position, sometimes taking a short ball, sometimes drifting wide, occasionally staying in an orthodox position. The third player should attempt to move the ball without hesitancy to the new position of his winger.

Exercise 3

The players line up one metre apart, one behind the other. As the ball is fed to the first man, each player in turn swings wide in an arc to run straight to receive the ball running parallel with the touch line, attempt to move the ball in a stride to the receiver. Players should be running straight before they receive the ball with the hands out towards the passer of the ball.

Exercise 4

Players line up one metre behind each other but also one metre to the side of each other. Again the players are running straight taking the ball early and moving the ball in a stride. Encourage the players to accelerate *before* they receive the ball in their hands and to move it in a stride.

Exercise 5

Toe the line. Players line up as in Fig 97. The two scrum-halves are static. Each line in turn passes the ball quickly while running forward to toe the line, after passing they re-align ready to repeat the exercise. The first passer loops to receive the final pass with all the others regrouping. Players should keep their depth in order to complete all the passes.

Exercise 6

In groups of six, using the techniques practised previously, i.e. pass the ball to the hands, run straight slightly at the inside shoulder of the defenders. The attackers now work against a more active defence. The defenders approach from the side as the ball is fed to the first man, each attacking player in turn straightens his line of running to check the defender before passing the ball to the man outside him. Players constantly change positions.

Exercise 7

Six attacking players against five defenders: the defending players follow the coach around the field and are grouped tightly together *(Fig 98)*. As soon as the ball is passed to the attacking scrum-half, the defenders will leave their position and fan out to try to stop the ball getting to the wing. The attacking side are again implementing the skills already learned by straightening their line of running, stopping defenders moving across the field as they pass the ball. If a defender does continue across then he is open for the dummy pass; the players react exactly as they would in a game situation. At every breakdown or score the ball is returned immediately to the coach, the defenders re-group behind the coach and play becomes continuous.

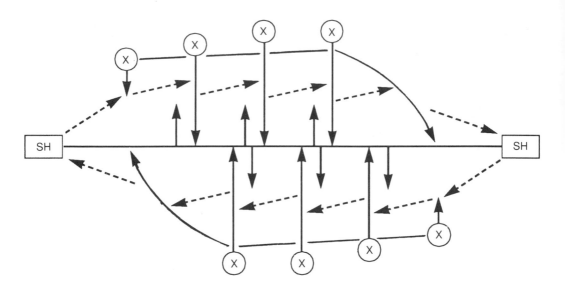

Fig 97   Toe the line drill.

Fig 98   Jeremy Guscott (Bath and
England) attacking his opponents' threequarter line.

ATTACK

For any threequarter line to be successful in attack, they must have an appreciation of what the defending side will attempt to do, and work out ways of overcoming them. Again there are no simple rules which apply to all situations but I think it is possible to set out some general principles.

Scrum Ball

From a scrum we can generally assume that the defending side will line up as close to the offside line (hindmost foot of the scrum) as possible and will sprint up in line to pressurise the side with the ball. The most vulnerable area therefore will be around the outside-half and the two centres *(Fig 99)*. The attacking side must hold the defenders in this area and move the ball to players with more time and space to attack. The blind-side wing can act as a decoy runner appearing on the shoulder of the outside-half or inside centre. This will prevent the defending side from covering across the field early thus cutting out moves. A dummy scissor move between outside-half and inside centre or the two centres has the same effect. These decoy moves followed immediately by a miss pass – outside-half to outside centre or inside centre to the full-back entering the line wide out will change the focus of attack before the defence has time to adjust.

Line-out Ball

At line-outs the threequarter lines will start at least twenty metres apart. This gives the defending side more time in which to react to

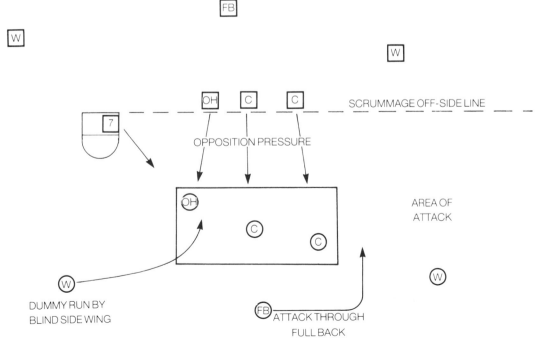

Fig 99   Threequarter attack from a scrum ball.

ploys carried out by the attacking team. As the ball moves along the line, so the defending side will try to adjust their positions in order to cover the entry of extra men into the line. The defensive pressure will therefore focus around the outside centre and wing.

The attacking side can encourage their opponents to drift across the field by using a miss pass – the defenders will follow the ball. A change of direction is then necessary in order to exploit the defensive drift. This can be a switch between the outside centre and wing or full-back, or merely an inside pass to the player missed out initially. The attack is running slightly infield on the weaker inside shoulder of the defending players.

Ruck and Maul

It is more difficult to lay down principles from rucks and maul. The defending side may have players committed to a tackle or the attacking side may have a threequarter involved in a ruck or maul. The necessity is for *all* threequarters to use their eyes to make a quick assessment of the opponents' line up and to attack at the weakest point. This may well involve players moving to replace a trapped colleague, for example wing moving to centre, but all players must react quickly to exploit the situation before the defence has time to re-organise.

Practices for a Threequarter Line

Exercise 1

A scrum-half with six rugby balls should be positioned on the half-way line five metres in from touch with his threequarters aligned outside him. The ball is passed from right to left in the first instance with the full-back joining the line as an extra man. When the winger gets the

ball he rolls it away, the whole threequarter line re-aligns to come back in the opposite direction, this time passing the ball off the left hand. The wingers change over each time. The full back would be expected to join the line on each alternate run; this exercise is repeated six times. The key coaching points are that the ball must be passed in one stride, and the players are encouraged to maintain their alignment and not to creep forward before they receive the ball. This is a good exercise to maintain discipline in position, alignment and passing of the ball. The aim is to complete six movements without dropping the ball. If the ball is dropped at any time the players should ignore it and re-align for the next pass as they would do had the movement been successfully completed.

Exercise 2 (Fig 100)

The players pass the ball from different positions moving up the field. Starting on the left-hand side of the 22 metre line, the ball is moved along the threequarter line with every player looping in support until they cross the first 10 metre line; continuing in the same direction the players re-align to play off a ball situated on the right-hand side of the 10 metre line, the exercise being repeated until all the players have crossed the next 10 metre line. They re-align moving in the same direction to play off a ball on the left-hand side of the 10 metre line, each player passing and looping in support until the 22 metre line is passed by all the players. They then re-align to play off a ball from the right-hand side of that 22 metre line to score over the goal-line. On each occasion the players are given sufficient time to re-align themselves and dispose of the ball before the next ball is moved to the scrum-half. The same coaching points as in the first exercise should be emphasised.

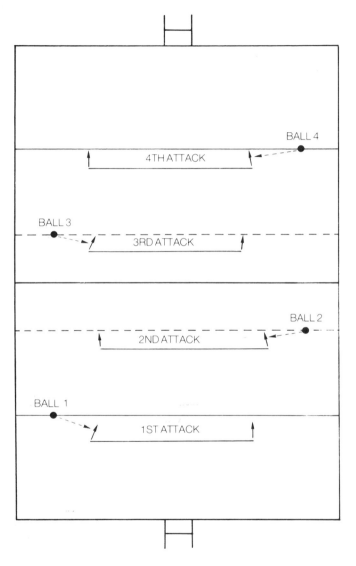

BALL 4

4TH ATTACK

BALL 3

3RD ATTACK

BALL 2

2ND ATTACK

BALL 1

1ST ATTACK

Fig 100   Practice for threequarter line –
four starting positions.

Exercise 3 (Fig 101)

The emphasis is on the outside half and two centres passing the ball very quickly and accurately, with a full back and wing injecting pace into the move by timing their runs from a deep position. From the starting position shown in Fig 101, the ball is passed quickly from scrum-half through all the hands to outside centre, the full back and wing time their run to appear outside the centre to continue the movement at

The Threequarters

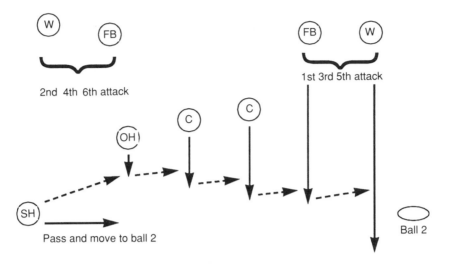

Fig 101 Practices for a threequarter line –
injection of pace.

pace. The outside half and two centres immediately reform from the other side and continue on the coach's count of one, two, three, this time with a different full back and wing. Six repetitions is the aim with no mistakes.

Exercise 4

The threequarter line works in conjunction with a back row. The ball is moved from the scrum-half along the threequarter line to the far winger who places the ball on the ground having sprinted forward fifteen to twenty metres. The back row follow across the field, pick the ball up and attack in the opposite direction until they have made *six* passes between them, at which time the ball is produced to the scrum-half and the backs continue the attack. As soon as the ball reaches the winger again, after sprinting fifteen to twenty metres he places it on the floor, the

back row have sprinted across the field, picked the ball up to attack in the opposite direction, this time completing *five* passes before the ball is produced to the scrum-half at which time the backs must have re-aligned to attack in the same direction as the back row. This exercise is repeated with the back row making *four* passes, *three* passes, *two* passes and finally just *one* pass before the ball is presented to the scrum-half. This means that the threequarters will have less time on each occasion in which to re-align and will mean that players may have to interchange positions, for example if there is insufficient time for the outside-half to get into position, his place may have to be taken by the blind-side winger and the outside-half may well find himself running as a centre threequarter. Each player must react according to the calls of the players round him. The object is, if possible, to complete all six attacks without dropping the ball.

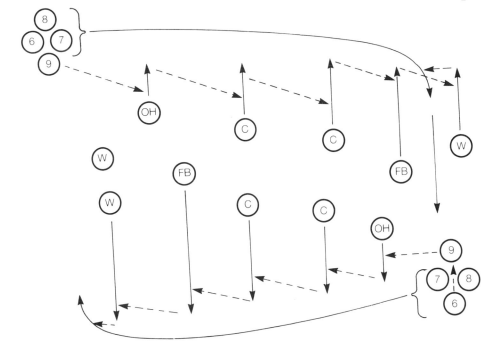

*Fig 102   Practice for threequarters and back
            row.*

Exercise 5

The coach, positioned on the 22 metre line with the ball, has a threequarter line on either side of him *(Fig 103)*. He will move backwards and forwards across the 22 metre line to be followed by each scrum-half. The rest of the threequarters will adjust their positions according to the movement of the coach. At any time the ball could be given to either scrum-half and the threequarter lines react either to attack with the ball or to become defenders. As soon as the move breaks down or a try is scored, the ball is passed back to the coach who continues his movements backwards and forwards across the 22 metre line posing problems for both sides. The object of this practice is for the players to react to the defensive alignment of their opposite numbers and if possible create an overlap by moving the ball quickly to a man in space or running in support of the ball carrier.

DEFENCE

A great deal of time in practice is spent working on the use of the ball in attacking situations. When one considers that in an evenly contested match the opposition will be in possession of the ball for 50 per cent of the game, it shows the importance of a well organised defence to any team. The features of any well organised defence will be that they arrive quickly and in numbers, they will all be sure in the tackle, and they will pressure their opposite numbers, forcing errors. In order for this to happen, all members of the threequarter line should be aware of their role at any particular situation and they must all work together.

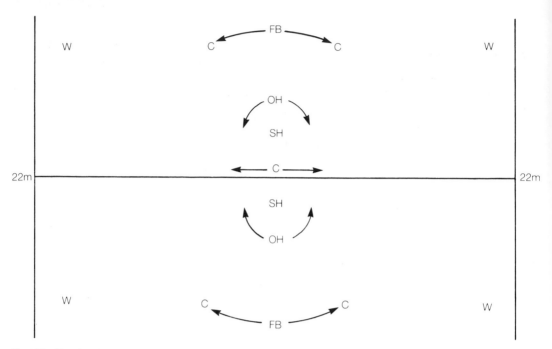

Fig 103 Practice for threequarter lines.

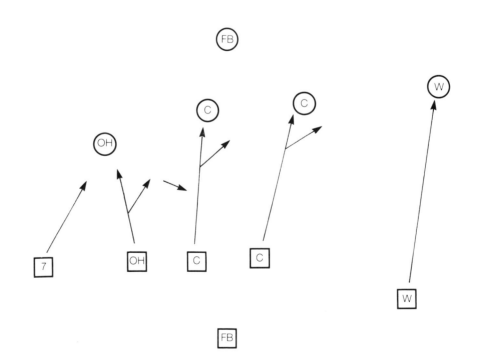

Fig 104 The threequarters in defence.

Basic Rules

1. Each player stays on the inside shoulder of his opposite number aiming to force him across the field. The exception is the outside-half who will stay slightly on the outside of his opposite number from the scrummage; the open side flanker will take the inside line on the opposition outside-half *(Fig 104).*

2. When the opposition have passed the ball it is essential that the player covers the inside shoulder of the next ball carrier to cover any change of direction, for example, a switch move.

3. When the ball has moved on, add depth by sweeping behind the rest of the backs.

4. If an extra man is brought in to the three-quarter line, for example, the full-back between the outside centre and the wing, the defending winger will move infield to tackle the full-back, with the defending full-back sweeping across the field to take the winger on the overlap. The blind-side wing should be covering infield to take the full-back's position *(Fig 105).*

5. From a line-out the flanker at the end of the line will take the opposing outside half. This allows the defending outside half to take the opposing inside centre with the rest of the threequarters also defending 'one out'. Thus any extra attaching player is covered, with the full back still available as an extra defender. Points two and three above still apply.

6. The outside-half and the two centres will position themselves no further than two metres apart and as close to the offside line as they can, and will move forward at the speed

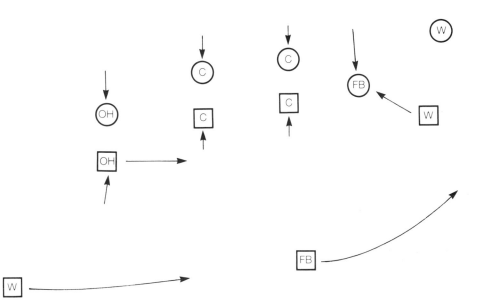

Fig 105 Threequarter defence to full-back entering the line.

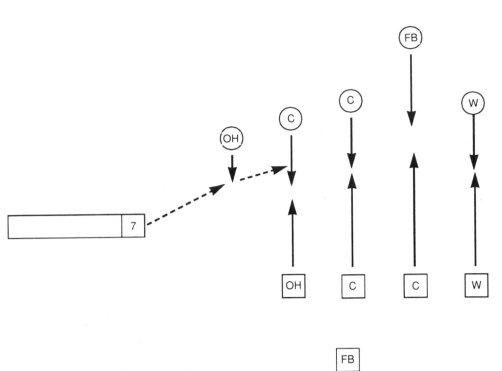

Fig 106   Threequarter defence from the line-out.

of the slowest man. Under no circumstances should one player attempt to go up more quickly on his man, as this will create a dogleg defence for the opposition to exploit.

A set of threequarters should practise their defensive positions for the ball being moved wide on the overlap with the addition of an extra man to the threequarter line, and also to cover any changes of direction (switch plays) bringing the ball back infield. It is also important that they work with their back row in order to establish their patterns of defensive play.

SUMMARY

With the threequarters, work on individual skills is paramount. The players must master all the passing variations; they must be able to handle the ball consistently and to pass quickly when under pressure. Players must be encouraged to pass the ball into the hands of the receiver so that the person receiving the ball is in a position to use it quickly. Straight running in all practices is essential to combat the modern tendency to drift sideways across the field.

All threequarters must be confident in tackling their opponents in a variety of ways. The half-backs must spend a lot of time practising the front tackle, but other threequarters will find themselves confronted by players running at them from a variety of angles and therefore must be able to master all types of tackle. Time should be spent on kicking, particularly the grubber kick, putting the ball behind the opposition's defence, and the punt which may be used to clear the lines in defence or to gain a position from which to launch an attack.

The half-backs must be aware of the importance of their play to the rest of the threequarter line: any weaknesses here will make it extremely difficult for the threequarter line to function as an efficient unit. All threequarters must be aware of the importance of the gain and tackle lines and should develop methods of crossing the gain line.

Decision making games are an important part of the coaching of threequarters. Players can be divided into small teams playing in a defined part of the field, and should be encouraged to use their handling variations to support the ball carrier, to read their opponent's movements, to react with a counterattack at the weakest point and to score. These games are valuable in testing the development of the players' technique and their ability to make the *correct decisions* in a game-like situation. They provide the necessary variety in a coaching session and are most enjoyable for those participating.

I would encourage the threequarters to spend as much time as possible developing their individual skills, to spend less time practising kicking at goal and more time handling the ball until they become very confident and adept. The coach should spend less time working with the unit as a whole and more time in small-sided games where the individual development of each player can be encouraged. Coaching of the threequarters is a most enjoyable part of rugby football but does require the coach to think about what he is doing and to develop relevant activities. Running with the ball is the most thrilling part of the game and all players, but most especially the threequarters, should be given the confidence to run with the ball at every opportunity.

SUMMARY

1. All threequarters *must* work hard at individual skills; passing and tackling are particularly important.
2. Good half-backs make a threequarter line.
3. Use decision making practices to encourage good decisions in matches.
4. A threequarter line should practise defence as well as attack, after all, the opposing team is likely to have possession of the ball for about half the game.
5. A repertoire of set moves should be developed to pose a series of attacking threats to the opposition, but players should not forget the importance of an individual taking on his opposite number, or of two players working together using a variety of running angles and short and long passes to breach the defence.

5 Team Practice

Having prepared the individuals and the units, the team should work together as a whole, at least for a short period of time in each coaching session. The coach will have his own ideas about the type of game he would like the team to play. The fifteen players involved should work together to practise the coach's ideas and to establish their general principles of play. This is an opportunity for the team to work on the pattern of game which they would like to use in the following match, to improve communication between individual players and the units, to work on their lines of support and to establish their priorities for use of the ball.

PRINCIPLES OF PLAY

In order to develop a successful side everybody must go onto the field knowing exactly what their role is and what should happen in the team effort. The basic principles of play in rugby football are:

1. Go forward.
2. Support (the ball carrier).
3. Continuity (keeping the ball alive).
4. Pressure (the opposition).

Go Forward

In order to gain ground in rugby football the ball carrier must take the most direct route to the opponents' goal-line. He must go forward. The temptation for young players is to run away from the opposition and into the wide open spaces, often running behind team-mates in the process. This makes it very difficult for his team-mates to follow and to give him the necessary support. We must go forward, not only in open play when running with the ball but also when winning the ball. The scrummage should be going forward at the moment the ball is presented to the scrum-half, the line-out should win the ball going forward, and certainly rucks and mauls should present the ball to the scrum-half while the forwards are still driving with their opposition in retreat. If this ideal position could be achieved, how simple the game would be! Nevertheless, the players must be instilled with the idea that at every possible opportunity, if nothing else, they must go forward with the ball.

Support

Support begins immediately the referee's whistle is blown for the start of the game. The player catching the kick-off must receive the support of the nearest forwards in order to protect him and the ball from the opposition and ensure that possession is retained for his side. In the scrummage, eight individuals will be less effective than one unit of eight supporting and working together to ensure that the hooker has maximum opportunity to win the ball for his side. Similarly, in the line-out the jumper on his own is ineffective unless he has the co-operation of the player throwing the ball in and the players on either side of him. Having won the ball, the role of the forwards is then to support the threequarters so that if a movement breaks down they are on hand before the opposition in order to lend support and retain possession for their side. The three-quarters should be aiming to cross the gain line to make the lines of running of the forwards that much easier. The forwards should know in which direction the attack is being mounted once the ball has been won.

Continuity

Having gained possession of the ball, the opposition must be denied the opportunity of regaining it; this can be achieved by well organised unit play in the rucks and mauls but also by skilful use of the ball in the hand. A well-timed pass, the ability to beat an opponent, or to regain possession when the ball is on the floor or in the air, are all important skills which will lend continuity to the game. Nothing is more frustrating for a side than, having lost the ball, being denied further possession by their opponents' skilful play.

Pressure

Having lost possession of the ball, the opposition should be given as little opportunity as possible to create scoring opportunities. This may be done in a number of ways, forwards increasingly putting pressure on the opposition at the scrum or the line-out so that, although possession may be won, it will be won going backwards and if possible disrupted. The threequarters and back row must put maximum pressure on the opposition in the tackle, making sure that their defence is rock solid thus giving few opportunities for the opposition to create a score. All of these things will create an atmosphere in which it will be difficult for your opponents to play with the freedom which they desire. Mistakes will occur allowing possession of the ball to be regained.

Communication

For a team to function smoothly, it is vital that everyone knows exactly what is going to happen at every phase of the game. Forwards need to know in which direction play is going after the ball is won from a set piece. This is usually relayed to the forwards via the scrum-half, eg. as he prepares to put the ball into a scrum he may call 'ready greens' to signify a right hand attack or 'ready cov' for a left side attack.

The back row will need more detail in order to beat their opposite numbers to the breakdown. A code to signify in which area of the field the attack will go, left, middle, right, but also the name or number of the player carrying out the strike will prove useful.

The forward and back units will develop their own calls for line-outs, back row moves from the scrum, and for threequarter moves, but they must be aware of team calls in order for each unit to support the other.

During team practice sessions the coach should set up the attacking situations, but leave the players to call the moves once the patterns of play and the calls have been established. This is good practice for those players responsible for decision making in the games.

PRACTICE METHODS

Unopposed Practices

One of the easiest methods of impressing upon a side the principles of play and the patterns which the coach would like to see them produce in a match is to practise with no opposition. This will help develop confidence, as the team will be able to run through their whole repertoire of moves in the knowledge that there are no opponents in the way to cause problems. Well run unopposed rugby practice is a good way of obtaining a high level of fitness, but the players must be disciplined not to cheat. It is too easy in unopposed rugby for forwards to take a short cut across the field or to leave a scrum or line-out earlier than they would in a match, thus creating a false impression of the speed in which they will arrive in support of other players. Here are five examples of unopposed rugby sequences which will serve as a basis for coaches to work out similar progressions of their own.

Line-out on the Defensive 10 metre Line

The ball is won from the line-out and fed along the threequarter line. After passing the ball, the threequarters support the ball carrier until the arrival of the back row and the forwards. The forwards will handle the ball interpassing until the signal from the pack leader for the ruck. The ball is rucked quickly to the scrum-half, transferred to the backs who handle, support and score.

Kick-off

The team receives a kick-off; after a tidy maul, an attack is mounted down the blind side using the back row, the scrum-half and the blind-side wing. The ball is rucked quickly to the backs who attack the open side, the threequarters support each other as in exercise 1 until the forwards arrive. The forwards interpass and at this stage passes must alternately be made to a forward and a back to encourage all fifteen players to run in support until a try is scored.

Scrum on the Half-way Line

A scrum fifteen metres in from touch on the half-way line – a back row move to the open side to produce a driving maul, the ball being produced for the backs to interpass and score. The decision as to whether to continue to attack in the same direction as the back row move or to move back in the opposite direction is left to the half-backs.

Scrum on the Attacking 10 metre Line

A mid-field scrum on the attacking 10 metre line. Back row move going right, back row and scrum-half support and interpass, the ruck is formed, the backs are given quick ball to run, handle and score.

Line-out Peel

A line-out peel from a line-out on the attacking 10 metre line into the mid-field. Again the half-backs have the option to attack in the same direction or to work back towards the touch-line, the forwards support, producing ·quick ruck ball for the threequarters to handle and score.

Semi-opposed Practices

As with individual and unit skills, having established the patterns of play, the pressure should be increased by adding opposition to the part of the play which is being practised at any particular moment in time. The following are some examples.

Back Row Move

Any back row move from a scrummage will take place against an opposing back row, who would start off initially in a kneeling position, together with the half-backs, the scrum-half standing in the normal position from a scrummage, and the outside-half adopting his normal set piece position. The attacking players are therefore confronted with the sort of defence that they will meet in a game and work their support against it.

Line-out

The line-out peel would be opposed by the opposition back row who would compete for the ball initially and then defend against the first players round the line-out as in a normal game. The opposition scrum-half, outside-half and inside centre can be added as this is the area the forwards will attack should the peel be successful.

Short Penalty Moves

Short penalty moves would be pressurised by opposition against the ball carrier, a post player if there is one, and the first runners with the ball. This again encourages the attacking side to support the ball carrier rather than watch the move from a distance.

Threequarters

The threequarters could work throughout a session against their mid-field opposite numbers, the half-backs and the two centres. The object throughout the practice would be for them to exploit the overlap by running straight and timing the pass.

Random Defence

A random defence. The opposition are given four or five forwards and four or five backs, the defenders are told to get in the way, to pop up in unusual positions, and the attacking side reacts to them and adjusts their play accordingly.

Unit Versus Unit Practices

A coach may be presented with a situation where he only has fifteen or twenty players with which to work. Having run through some unopposed practices he may well wish to pressurise his players rather more fully. This can be done by playing one unit against another in a number of ways.

Line-out (Fig 107)

From a line-out the forwards win the ball and present it to the scrum-half. As soon as the ball is moved away to the threequarters, the forwards become opposition and defend the attacking movement of the backs. This gives the coach the opportunity firstly to check on the defensive lines of running of his back row and the rest of the forwards, and secondly to see how quickly the threequarters are able to move the ball away from the pressure of the forwards at the line-out.

Line-out Peel

The forwards peel from the back of the line-out, any spare man giving immediate opposition; the peel is then continued into the mid-field, where the threequarters defend and, if they are able to win possession of the ball, launch a counter attack.

Scrum (Fig 108)

A scrum in mid-field, on the 10 metre line. The forwards win the ball from the scrummage facing the posts and the threequarter line. The scrum-half puts up a high kick ahead which is chased by the forwards when they are put on side by the scrum-half. The threequarters catch the kick and launch a counter attack aiming to score over the half-way line against the forwards.

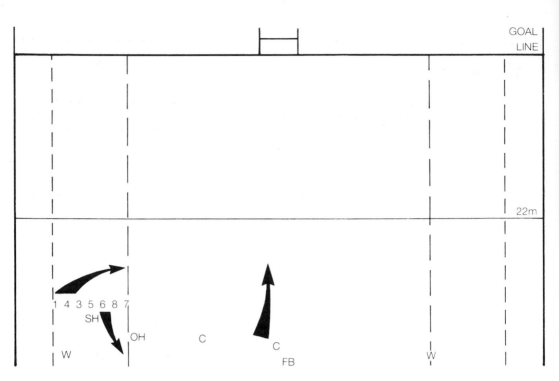

Fig 107   Unit against unit practice from line-
out.

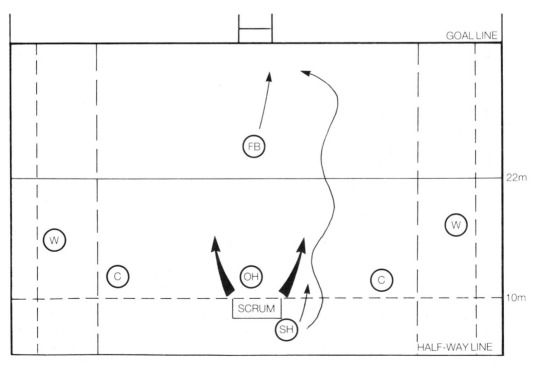

Fig 108   Unit against unit practice from
midfield scrum.

SUMMARY

Team practice is vital in pulling together the individuals and units into a well rehearsed team prior to a match. It provides an opportunity to blend the two units together, to establish priorities and build team confidence by running patterns of play.

1. Confirm and establish the patterns of play.
2. Build team communication via the half-backs. Who has priority in certain situations – forwards or backs?
3. Use a variety of team practice methods to pressure different units, working as close to game pace as possible.
4. Avoid long or frequent discussions – do the talking before or after the session.
5. Always try to finish on a positive note – don't go on too long!

Back Row Move

A back row move; the backs again defend this move with any spare men acting as back row forwards and again if they are able to win possession of the ball, launch a counter attack to score.

Conditioned Game

A conditioned game allows the team the opportunity to practise against full opposition. The coach should control the game throughout in order that the practice is a constructive one. It is an opportunity to practise set positions and the options available to the team both in attack and defence and to allow these positions to be repeated time and time again.

A conditioned game should be run over a series of short time periods, perhaps ten to fifteen minutes of action followed by a rest during which time the coach and players will talk about what has been happening, the problems that have arisen and the ways of solving them during the next short period of play. Some examples of conditions which might be imposed in a conditioned game are:

1. Every restart from a breakdown in play could be (a) from a scrum (b) from a line-out, or (c) a short penalty, according to the emphasis of the training session.
2. From every scrum a back row move must be the first priority.
3. The side in possession must kick the ball from half-back, allowing the opposition practise at the counter attack.
4. The ball when transferred to the threequarter line of one side must be used in a switch move thus allowing the opposition to practise their defence against such moves.
5. A continuous session of 5 metre scrums, allowing the teams to practise both their attacking options and how to defend from such situations.

Once the condition has been established, the game continues until the next breakdown and then restarts in whatever manner the coach has decided needs to be practised during that particular period of time. This allows for the side to work continuously at one particular aspect of their game against full opposition, to experience the likely problems which will be met in a game and to practise ways of overcoming them. All teams should practise at some stage against full opposition.

6 Fitness

Fitness is an essential aspect of team preparation. Much of the work with individuals, units and indeed the full team can contain an element of fitness training; it is essential that it does because the amount of time left specifically for the physical preparation of players is often quite small. Variety is an important aspect of fitness work. Players enjoy a change of activity and will respond with enthusiasm to a slightly new approach to fitness work. A visit from a local athletics coach can give a different approach to speed and stamina training. An assault/obstacle course can be constructed cheaply by club members. This can be used as part of the organised club training or by the keener players as extra work. Some clubs have produced their own weight training apparatus using hinged scaffold poles, weighted paint drums and concrete blocks or metal bars. Some ingenuity on the part of club members will usually lead to the production of the type of apparatus the club coach feels is a useful addition to the training facilities.

SKILLS CIRCUIT

A skills circuit will involve the players in a repetition of the skills of the game being reproduced quickly, in a small area, usually against a time limit. The circuit can be organised around a grid area, the players working in groups of four, two working, two resting in turn before they move on to the next exercise (Fig 109). In some cases the resting pair will act as opposition or feeders of the ball.

Exercises

Two-handed Jump

Rugby balls suspended from the cross bar of the goal post at various heights to suit the tall and short players. The players continually leap into the air and touch the rugby ball with two hands.

Tackling

A tackle bag is placed in the centre of a ten metre grid and each player of the pair runs to tackle the tackle bag and continues to the far side of the grid ready to complete a second tackle on the return journey. The two resting players are responsible for replacing the tackle bag after each tackle.

The Switch Pass

Two players with one ball at one side of the grid move forward, complete a switch pass and run to the far side of the grid where they return and repeat the exercise.

Scrum-half Dive Pass

Two players situated in opposite corners of the grid, one player with a ball. He executes a scrum-half dive pass to his partner at the opposite side of the grid who catches the ball, places it on the floor and dive passes back to the first player. The exercise is continuous.

Fig 109   *Rugby skills circuit.*

Fitness

Picking up the Ball

The ball is situated approximately three metres into the grid; the first player runs across the grid, picks the ball up and puts it down before he reaches the far side of the grid, touches the end line and repeats the activity on the way back before touching his partner who continues with the same activity.

Mauling

The two resting players are situated on opposite sides of the grid. The first active player passes the ball across the grid, runs across and fights to maul the ball away from the opposition; the aim is for him to work for approximately five seconds – he then passes the ball back across the grid to the second player, runs across, mauls the ball off him and feeds it to his partner who completes the exercise. The players continue for a specified time.

Fall and Roll

To improve contact with the ground. The two resting players adopt a position on their hands and knees across the grid. The two working players in turn will dive over each body and roll to his feet. The players work continuously.

The Lateral Pass

The two resting players position themselves at opposite corners of the grid, approximately two metres from the end line. One player has a ball, the two working players will shuttle backwards and forwards across the grid. The first player receives a pass from the resting player with the ball, passes it to his partner who gives the ball to the next resting player on the far side of the grid. Players run to the end line, turn and repeat the exercise coming back.

Torpedo Throw and Catch

Each player in turn acts as a thrower of the ball or a catcher. The player with the ball makes a torpedo throw to his partner who must catch the ball in two hands while in the air. He then becomes the thrower, and his partner takes on the role of a catcher. For the exercise to be valid, the ball must be caught cleanly while the player is in the air.

Scrummaging One Versus One

One player acts as a locked scrummager and the other one with bent legs attempts to push his partner backwards. After approximately five seconds they change roles.

The players can either work for a specified period of time, for example thirty seconds on each exercise, or until they complete a specified number of repetitions, for example ten or fifteen. The resting players act as referees and scorer for the two who are working. Players should obtain a score for each exercise completed and a total score for the completed circuit. This adds a competitive and enjoyable element to the skills circuit. It is possible for the coach to substitute other exercises.

THE FITNESS CIRCUIT

An exercise circuit is useful in that it can be adapted for use either indoors in a gymnasium or sports hall or outside on the field. Many exercises are well known but the coach should take into account the need to include some flexibility and mobility exercises as well as pure strength.

Exercises

Press-ups

There are a variety of ways of doing the press-up in addition to the conventional one. The arms can be placed wide apart or closer together, ultimately with one hand on top of the other. By raising the legs, additional pressure can be put onto the arms.

Sit-ups

Again, there are a variety of ways of doing sit-ups in addition to the common one where the legs are kept straight and the elbows are brought over to touch the knees. Legs can be split wide apart and the right elbow is brought across to touch the left knee, the left elbow to touch the right knee on each repetition. The legs start on the floor and as the trunk raises so the knees come up to touch the elbows forming a vee-sit position.

Knees to the Chest

The player from standing position jumps into the air raising his knees to touch his chest, straightens his legs to touch the floor again and immediately springs up to complete the exercise again.

A Star Jump

From a crouch position with hands on the floor the player springs into the air, stretches his hands and feet wide to form a star before landing in the squat position again.

Burpees

From a standing position – the player crouches with his hands touching the floor; from this crouch position the legs are ex-tended fully backwards, they are then brought back again to the crouch position from where the player jumps high in the air extending his arms above his head. The exercise is completed as quickly as possible on each occasion.

Squat Thrusts

From a press-up position the knees are bent and brought up to a position level with the elbows and then the legs are extended fully out behind the player. Again the exercise is completed as quickly as possible.

Vee Sits

The player lies on his back with his arms extended over his head and raises his trunk and arms and his legs to touch in the air above his head in a vee position and then reverts to a prone position on the floor.

Back Bends

The player lies on his stomach, the hands can either be clasped behind his head raised at shoulder height on either side of the body or clasped behind the back. To complete the exercise the player raises his chest off the floor, lifting the head as high as possible and at the same time lifting the legs off the floor. Return to the original position to complete the exercise.

Bridging

From a position lying on the back with the knees bent, feet flat on the floor the player will form a bridge, his body being supported between his head and his feet. This is a neck-strengthening exercise.

Fitness

Leg Raised Cycling

From lying on his back the player will roll up onto his shoulders, supporting his body with his arms and from this position will execute a cycling movement with his legs in the air.

Legs Raised

From a prone position lying on his back, the player will raise his legs twelve inches off the ground and from this position can perform a variety of exercises, either a splits where his legs are opened wide and then closed together again, or the legs crossing continuously, left leg over right followed by right leg over left, etc. At no time should the legs touch the floor.

Splits over Head

Player adopts a starting position for the cycling exercise but from this position the legs are open wide to form a vee position between the legs and then closed together again. The legs can be split either side to side or forward and backwards.

Alternate Overhead Leg Touch

From a prone position on the floor the player rolls backwards to touch the ground behind his head with first of all his right leg, returns to the starting position and repeats the exercise with his left leg.

Leg to Alternate Hands

Player lies on his back in crucifix position, the right leg is extended across his body to touch his left hand and returned to starting position. The left leg then rotates across the body to touch the right hand and return to its starting position.

As for the skills circuit, the fitness circuit can either take the form of a set number of repetitions before the player moves on to the next exercise or to exercise continually for a period of time – fifteen to thirty seconds is suggested. The range of exercises can be extended if the club or school is fortunate enough to have some apparatus available.

RUNNING EXERCISES
(Figs 110 to 113)

Although players will do some running as part of the skills training using a rugby ball, there is a case to be made for running without a ball for the improvement of speed or stamina.

Shuttle Runs

The players will run between two lines ten metres apart completing ten runs, making a total of 100 metres on each occasion. The players will touch each line with their hand before turning for the next sprint. After completion of the ten lengths, a one minute rest period is given and the players should repeat the exercise six times initially, building up as fitness improves to a maximum of ten runs of 100 metres. By using shuttle exercises a great deal of running can be completed in a short period of time. Shuttle running has been shown as a good method of improving fitness quickly.

Runs using the Rugby Pitch

The pitch can be used in a variety of ways to produce sprints and rest periods of differing lengths. Here are four suggestions:

1. Run from the corner of the pitch diagonally to the junction of the 22 metre line and the opposite touch-line, walk back to the goal-

line.
2. Run from the corner of the pitch diagonally to the junction of the half-way line and the opposite touch-line then walk on to the far goal-line.
3. Run from the corner of the pitch diagonally to the junction of the far 22 metre line and the opposite touch-line. Walk on to the original goal-line.
4. Run from one corner of the pitch to the other.

The players should run in groups with a suggested maximum of six players in each group. As all the groups complete one run, the first group is ready to complete the second run having had a reasonable period of rest. This complete circuit can be run on four to six occasions.

Using the outside of the pitch as a circuit, runs from 120 to 200 metres can be completed as follows:

1. Run from behind the goal posts around the corner flag and along the side of the pitch to the far goal-line: approximately 120 metres.
2. Run from one corner flag along the goal-line behind the goal posts round the next corner flag to complete a length of the pitch finishing at the far goal-line: approximately 140 metres.
3. Follow the same route but the starting point is from the 22 metre line: approximately 160 metres.
4. The same route starting from the half-way line: approximately 180 metres.
5. The same route starting from the far 22 metre line: approximately 200 metres.

As the distance that the players run increases, so the period allowed for their recovery decreases. The players, on completing their run, walk around the goal post at the far end and up the opposite touch line to complete a circuit of the pitch. I would advise that the backs run 120, 140, 160, 180, 200, 180, 160, 140 and 120 metres, but the forwards only run the 120 to 200.

For the final build-up to the season to sharpen sprinting speed and to improve agility, repetitions over shorter distances should be used. The emphasis is on speed off the mark and changes of direction. For examples, see page 116. Numerous relays involving picking up a stationary ball, changing direction or doing an exercise can also be used along with simple sprinting intervals. I hope these ideas will prompt club coaches to devise their own variations – players work harder when they enjoy what they are doing and they do enjoy variety.

SUMMARY

1. Although much fitness work can be built into the warm up and skills work some specific fitness training is vital.
2. Encourage players to do much of their fitness work away from the club, or before or after club sessions.
3. Produce a simple programme for pre-season work so that players arrive for the first club session in a reasonable state of fitness.
4. Variety is important. Further ideas can be obtained from *Fitness for Sport* (The Crowood Press, 1987).

Fitness

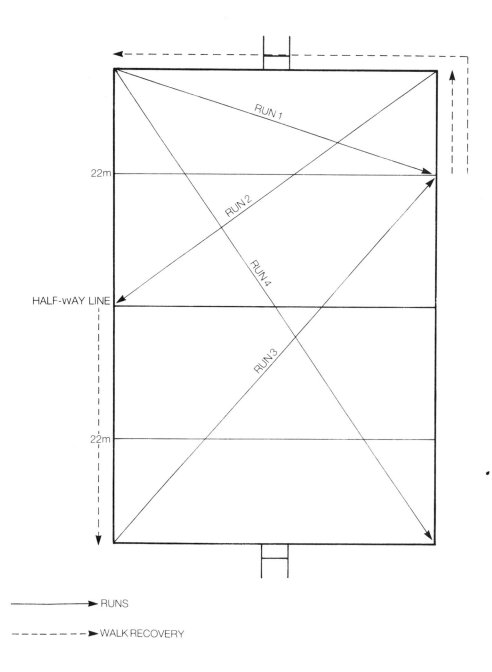

Fig 110   *Fitness runs across a rugby pitch.*

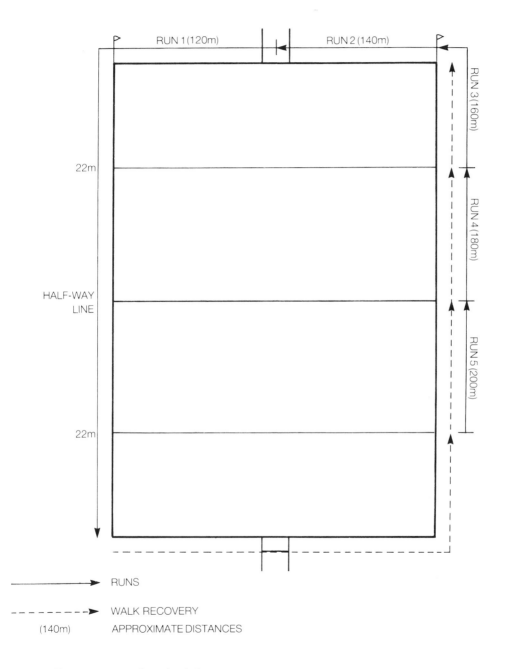

Fig 111   Fitness runs around a rugby pitch.

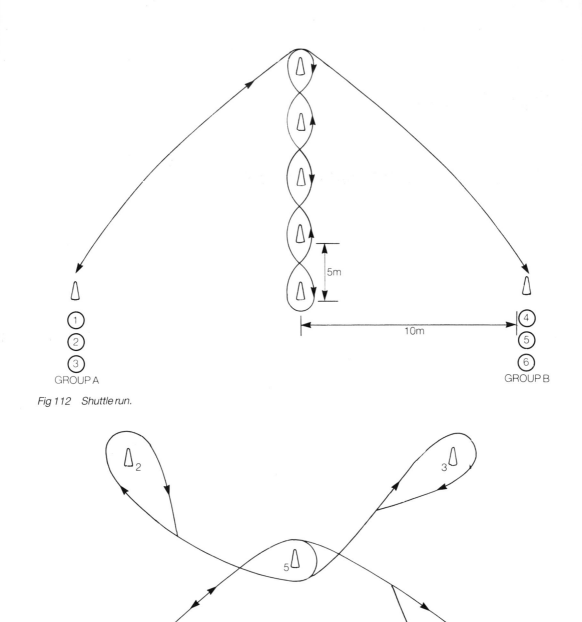

Fig 112   Shuttle run.

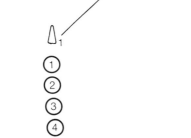

Fig 113   Agility run.

Appendix

PITCH AREAS FOR MINI-RUGBY

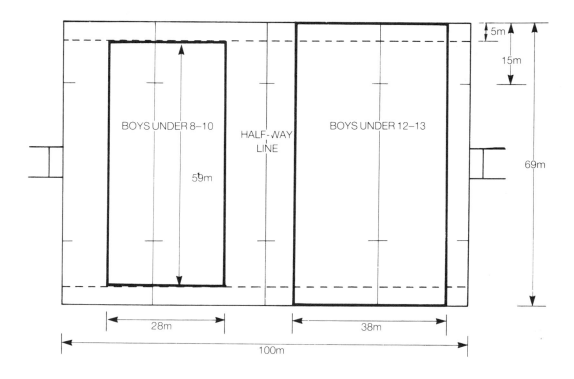

Useful Addresses

Keith Bonser
Divisional Technical Administrator
  (Midlands)
Gilberts of Rugby
5 St Matthew's Street
Rugby
Warwickshire

Tony Biscombe
Divisional Technical Administrator (North)
Morley RUFC
Scatcherd Lane
Morley
Leeds

Des Diamond
Divisional Technical Administrator
  (London)
North East London Polytechnic
Longbridge Road
Dagenham
Essex RM8 2AS

David Shaw
National Youth Development Officer
RFU Development & Resources Centre
Nortonthorpe Mills
Scissett
Huddersfield
HD8 9LA

Alan Black
National Promotions Officer
Rugby Football Union
Twickenham
Middlesex
TW1 1DZ

International Rugby Football Board
Avonbank
Clifton Down
Bristol BS8 3HT

Rugby Football Union
Twickenham
Middlesex TW1 1DZ

Federation Francaise de Rugby
7 Cite d'Antin
75009 Paris
France

Irish Rugby Football Union
62 Lansdowne Road
Dublin 4
Ireland

Scottish Rugby Union
Murrayfield
Edinburgh EH12 5PJ

Welsh Rugby Union
Cardiff Arms Park
PO Box 22
Cardiff CF1 1JL

Australian Rugby Football Union
PO Box 333
Kingsford
New South Wales 2023

New Zealand Rugby Football Union
PO Box 2172
Wellington 1
New Zealand

South African Rugby Football Union
PO Box 99
Newlands 7725
Cape Town
South Africa

Union Argentina de Rugby
J.A. Pacheco de Melo 2120
Cod Pos 1126 Capital
Buenos Aires
Argentina

Canadian Rugby Union
National Sport and Recreation Centre
1600 Prom. James Naismith Drive
Gloucester
Ontario K1B 5N4
Canada

Federazione Italiana Rugby
Via L Franchetti 2
00194 Rome
Italy

Japan Rugby Football Union
c/o Sanshin Enterprises Co.
Ichibancho Central Building
22-1 Chiyoda-Ku
Tokyo 102
Japan

United States of America Rugby Football
Union
3595 East Fountain Boulevard
Colorado Springs
CO 80910
USA

Index

Other Titles in The Skills of the Game Series

Further details of titles available or in preparation can be obtained from the publishers.